NEW FABIAN ESSAYS

NEW
FABIAN ESSAYS

R. H. S. Crossman   C. A. R. Crosland   Roy Jenkins
Margaret Cole   Austen Albu   Ian Mikardo
Denis Healey   John Strachey

Edited by R. H. S. Crossman

Preface by the Rt. Hon. C. R. Attlee

FREDERICK A. PRAEGER
NEW YORK

NEW
FABIAN ESSAYS

R. H. S. Crossman   C. A. R. Crosland   Roy Jenkins
Margaret Cole   Austen Albu   Ian Mikardo
Denis Healey   John Strachey

Edited by R. H. S. Crossman

Preface by the Rt. Hon. C. R. Attlee

FREDERICK A. PRAEGER
NEW YORK

'BOOKS THAT MATTER'

Published in the United States of America
in 1952 by
Frederick A. Praeger, Inc., Publishers,
105 West 40th Street, New York 18, N.Y.

Library of Congress Catalog Card No: 52-10784

Printed in Great Britain

CONTENTS

PAGE

Preface: The Rt. Hon. C. R. Attlee, O.M., C.H., M.P. vii

Introduction ix

TOWARDS A PHILOSOPHY OF SOCIALISM
R. H. S. Crossman 1

THE TRANSITION FROM CAPITALISM
C. A. R. Crosland 33

EQUALITY Roy Jenkins 69

EDUCATION AND SOCIAL DEMOCRACY
Margaret Cole 91

THE ORGANISATION OF INDUSTRY Austen Albu 121

TRADE UNIONS IN A FULL EMPLOYMENT
ECONOMY Ian Mikardo 143

POWER POLITICS AND THE LABOUR PARTY
Denis Healey 161

TASKS AND ACHIEVEMENT OF BRITISH LABOUR
John Strachey 181

v

PREFACE

SIXTY-THREE years ago the publication of FABIAN ESSAYS marked the beginning of a new approach to socialism. It was, in fact, the first clear statement of the philosophy of gradualism as against the Utopian or catastrophic ideas of the past. The British Labour and Socialist Movement has to a large extent lived on the thinking of the Fabian Essayists and their successors. Much of the programme which they envisaged has been carried out in Britain. The Welfare State in the stage which it has reached today is the result of the application of the doctrines of the FABIAN ESSAYS. The essayists did not give a blueprint for an ideal society. They recognised that society advances slowly and each advance brings with it new problems.

On the other hand, we have seen a thing which they did not anticipate; the putting into practice in Russia of the catastrophic theory with the results which we have to face today.

FABIAN ESSAYS were written in the climate of Victorian England. The reader today is struck by the almost complete absence of any reference to foreign affairs. There is an underlying assumption that peace will continue and will allow the development of socialism to take place in country after country. I welcome, therefore, this series of NEW FABIAN ESSAYS written by people of the younger generation who have grown up in the disturbed atmosphere of the twentieth century with the effects of two world wars vividly in mind.

They discuss socialist policy in the light of very different conditions from those obtaining in the days of their great predecessors. They are acutely aware of the impact on home problems of the international situation. They have to consider the future of Britain in the world of warring forces. The question which they have to answer is, 'Where do we go from here?'

The essays were planned in 1950 while the Labour Government was still in power and only one of the authors has had ministerial experience. I am glad to hear that a second series is planned and hope it will include essays by former members of the Labour Government. Their experience *would enable them to make useful contributions, especially in the realm of foreign affairs where some of the authors at times fall into the error of assuming that a British Foreign Minister has more freedom of action than he has.*

The essays should stimulate thought in the Movement. Several of them deal with the problem of making democracy effective in a society where managerial autocracy is an increasing danger. Mr. Albu and Mr. Mikardo are particularly interesting on this point. It is, however, not my business in a preface to deal with the individual essays or to weigh one against the other. All are well worth careful study and I commend NEW FABIAN ESSAYS *to our comrades not only in this country but overseas.*

C. R. ATTLEE

19th February, 1952

INTRODUCTION

EARLY in 1889 the Executive Committee of the Fabian Society issued its printed report for the Annual Business Meeting. In this modest, four-page document occurred an announcement that the course of lectures on *The Basis and Prospects of Socialism*, delivered in the previous autumn session, was to be published in book form. Edited by Bernard Shaw, these lectures formed *Fabian Essays*. Three hundred copies were subscribed for in advance; and when the prospective publisher refused to produce the book under fair trade conditions, the Fabian Society (which then had a little over a hundred members) published it at its own expense.

The result astonished all concerned. The first edition was sold out within a month; the second scarcely less rapidly; and through sixty years the demand continued (the final edition, issued in 1948, had no fewer than four Prefaces, as well as a postscript by Shaw). The exact number of copies sold is unknown, but it must run into hundreds of thousands; translations are too numerous to list.

This success certainly astonished the seven lecturers responsible for the Essays. When they composed them, they had no idea that they were contributing to a work of major political importance; nor did they conceive of themselves as the evangelists of a new brand of Fabian orthodoxy. Indeed, the small esteem in which they held themselves, and the meaning they gave to Fabianism, can be gauged from Shaw's original Preface:

Country readers may accept the book as a sample of the propaganda carried on by volunteer lecturers in the workmen's clubs and political associations of London.

And again:

Everything that is usually implied by the authorship and editing of a book has in this case been done by the seven essayists, associated in the Executive Council of the Fabian Society, and not one of the essays could be what it is had the writer been a stranger to his six colleagues and to the Society. But there has been no sacrifice of individuality—no attempt to cut out every phrase and opinion the responsibility for which would not be accepted by every one of the seven. . . . There are at present no authoritative teachers of Socialism. The essayists make no claim to be more than communicative learners.

These sentences express the spirit of Fabianism. They describe Fabians, first, as socialists; secondly, as colleagues collaborating to discover the best answers to insistent questions; thirdly, as individual thinkers, respecting one another's individuality; and, fourthly, as advisers rather than dogmatic politicians—'clerks to the Labour Movement', as Beatrice Webb put it. It is worth observing that the Fabian Society had been in existence for nearly five years—busily campaigning and pamphleteering for socialism—before it felt the necessity to formulate its ideas even in the undogmatic form of seven unconnected essays. This practical empiricism, which bases theory upon experience as well as upon group discussion, very largely accounts for the long-continued appeal of *Fabian Essays*.

But times change, and even the best empirically-based theories eventually get out of date. To the present generation of socialists, the detailed proposals and formulations of the original *Fabian Essays* can mean very little. Partly this is due to the achievements of the Labour Movement—Fabian blueprints for social welfare, redistributive taxation, nationalisation and national minima now form part of the law of the land; partly to changing social conditions (the trade unions, for instance, have altered enormously since Annie Besant wrote about them—before the first great dock strike). But partly the outdatedness of *Fabian Essays* derives from inadequacies in the original analysis. In 1952, for example, we realise that we cannot completely ignore the rest of the world, as our forbears did in 1889; nor can we accept the concept of a world automatically progressing towards expanding wealth and wider freedoms, which was so deeply rooted in Victorian thought that the first Fabians took it for granted without serious consideration.

Ever since the revival of the Fabian Society, which occurred in 1939, projects for a new series of Fabian Essays have been under discussion. The task was not an easy one. Not only are the problems of to-day more complex and far-reaching than those of sixty years ago; the information available—the sheer facts upon which policy must be grounded—have multiplied overwhelmingly. Moreover the modern Fabian, whose business it is to study and interpret those facts, has to spend much more time and energy earning his living than his predecessor, whose leisure-time propagandist activities Shaw described in his *Early History of the Fabian Society*. For these reasons, the first attempts at new Fabian Essays came to nothing. It was not until G. D. H. Cole—then Chairman of the Society—persuaded a group of Fabians to spend a week-end at Buscot Park in July, 1949, that a real start was made. The range of this first conference was very wide, including much argument on details; but then, rather unexpectedly, agreement was reached on the nature of the main problem. For two generations, socialist thought had been largely concentrated on the techniques for carrying out the programme envisaged in the original Essays and the expedients required to adapt that programme to the emergencies which had arisen. Comparatively little attention had been given to the structural changes in society which had been taking place and the new social sciences which were emerging. As a result, the election of the Labour Government in 1945, and the rapid completion of the Fabian programme, had been followed by a dangerous hiatus both of thought and action. It was not merely new expedients which were required, or new planks in an election programme, but a new analysis of the political, economic and social scene as a basis for reformulating socialist principles.

So conference succeeded conference; and, between conferences, papers were circulated on particular problems. There were withdrawals from the group. It lost some members owing to pressure of business; and one, the Chairman—to whose energy and inspiration the whole project was due—owing to a basic disagreement on policy. But, despite these losses, the unity of the group was successfully maintained; and, by the end of 1950, it became clear that some interim term must be set to all this intellectual activity. Everyone agreed that a comprehensive study of socialism was out of the question until much more work had been done. Time had returned on its spiral, and all that could be attempted was once again a series of individual essays in socialist thought. As Bernard Shaw said in 1889, 'There are at present no authoritative teachers of Socialism.' So the unity sought has been a unity of approach, not of specific opinions or propositions. The essayists have criticised one another, and been criticised by other members of the group, who have not contributed to the present series. It stands to reason that these latter, even less than the eight essayists, can be held committed to every line in the book. Nevertheless, as the eight authors would be the first to admit, this book is a product of Fabian group activity.[1]

A word about the individual essays. The eight subjects were selected, from a list of about twice that number, in order to achieve a balance between theoretical analysis and practical application. R. H. S. Crossman begins by an attempt to re-define the nature of Progress in a world which is certainly not progressing automatically towards social democracy; and then asks what changes in socialist attitudes are required in 'the century of totalitarianism.' C. A. R. Crosland follows with a new approach to 'post-capitalist economics,' analysing what has happened—in contrast with what Marx *said* would happen—to Western capitalism. Roy Jenkins, recognising equality as the concept which differentiates socialism from both liberalism and communism, examines the extent to which the aim of economic equalisation can be further pursued. Margaret Cole writes

[1] A list of members of the group is given at the end of this Introduction.

about education, which every socialist, from Robert Owen onwards, has recognised to be part of the foundation of any socialist society, but which formed the most glaring gap in the Labour Party's programme in 1945, 1950 and 1951. Austen Albu deals with the organisation of industry, and, in particular, with methods of bringing the private sector of industry under democratic control; and Ian Mikardo tackles the contentious issue of how the structure of trade unionism should be adapted to the requirements of a full-time economy. In the concluding sections, Denis Healey, faced perhaps with the most difficult task, tries to show what the methods of socialist foreign policy should be, now that it is clear that power politics cannot be 'abolished' either by disarmament or international machinery; and John Strachey, who has combined socialist theory with Cabinet experience, seeks to assess the changes achieved by the Labour Government as a basis on which to construct the next stage of socialism.

New Fabian Essays contains a good deal more historical background than the original volume. In the optimistic mood of the 1880's, the first Fabians took for granted both the shape of things past and the shape of things to come. We cannot write to-day without a much soberer consciousness of history, and a much more acute scepticism about the particular interpretation that we give it. In fact, we do not claim either finality or comprehensiveness for *New Fabian Essays*. Even the three years during which they were composed have brought changes which defied our predictions and warned us against ready-made conclusions. These essays, for instance, were written under a Labour Government, and revised in proof under a Tory Government. If they ask at least some of the new, pertinent questions, their authors will be content. And, in anticipation of what it believes to be the live and continuing interest of the Labour Movement, the Fabian Society has already started the group discussions for a second volume, which will both fill in gaps and open up new inquiries.

Meanwhile the eight essayists, not one of whom was alive at

the time when *Fabian Essays* appeared, can still find no better description of themselves than 'communicative learners.' If the problems of 1952 are different from those of 1889, we believe that the Fabian spirit is still essential to the cause of democratic socialism.

MARGARET COLE

R. H. S. CROSSMAN

The following is the list of the members of the group, out of whose discussions *New Fabian Essays* sprang:

Austen Albu, M.P. for Edmonton, author of *The Anatomy of Private Enterprise.*

Dr. N. Barou, author of *British Trade Unions.*

Ritchie Calder, Science Editor of the *News Chronicle.*

Donald Chapman, M.P. for Birmingham, Northfield, General Secretary of the Fabian Society.

Hugh Clegg, Fellow of Nuffield College, Oxford, and author of *Industrial Democracy and Nationalisation.*

Professor G. D. H. Cole.

Margaret Cole.

C. A. R. Crosland, M.P. for Gloucestershire, South.

R. H. S. Crossman, M.P. for Coventry, East.

Lord Faringdon, Chairman of the Fabian Colonial Bureau.

Allan Flanders, lecturer in Industrial Relations at Oxford University.

R. J. Goodman, Director of *Political and Economic Planning.*

H. D. Hughes, Principal of Ruskin College, Oxford.

Roy Jenkins, M.P. for Birmingham, Stechford.

Ian Mikardo, M.P. for Reading, South.

John Parker, M.P. for Dagenham, Chairman of the Fabian Society.

The Rt. Hon. Harold Wilson, M.P. for Lancaster, Huyton.

G. D. N. Worswick, Fellow of Magdalen College, Oxford.

Michael Young, Research Adviser to the Labour Party.

At a later stage, when authors for the essays were being selected, the group was joined by:

The Rt. Hon. John Strachey, M.P. for Dundee, West.

Denis Healey, at that time Secretary of the International Department of the Labour Party and now M.P. for Leeds, S.E.

TOWARDS A PHILOSOPHY OF SOCIALISM
R. H. S. Crossman

I. *The Loss of Momentum*

Even before the 1950 election, the impetus which brought the Labour Government to power began to fail. That impetus, despite a sharp setback in 1931, had mounted steadily during fifty years of opposition—years spent in a sustained campaign against the capitalist order. Yet, after scarcely four years in office, the Government had fulfilled its historic mission. The nationalisation of half a dozen major industries, the construction of an all-in system of social security and a free health service, and the tentative application of planning to the national economy—the achievement of these reforms seemed to have exhausted the content of British socialism.

What was the cause of this loss of political momentum? Not the deadlock result of the 1950 election—far less the need for rearmament after the attack on South Korea. Even if the Labour Government in 1950 had won a large parliamentary majority, the advance to socialism would have been halted. The right wing openly advocated consolidation; the left demanded more socialism, but could only suggest those measures required to achieve it. The rearmament programme (and the defeat at the polls in 1951) came as a deliverance from indecision, not as an obstacle to action.

It would be easy to attribute this indecision to a failure of leadership. Certainly, the almost simultaneous loss of his two strong men, Sir Stafford Cripps and Mr. Bevin, grievously weakened the Prime Minister's position and revealed a dangerous rift in his Cabinet. But these personal factors were symptoms of a much more serious ailment, a failure of the sense of direction which alone can unify and sustain a great political party. The Labour Party was unsure where it was going. The familiar landmarks on the road to socialism had been left behind: it was travelling in strange country, exposed to climatic rigours it had not anticipated and against which its traditional equipment gave little protection. Buffeted and battered, it pushed ahead; but the pace slowed as it became clear that the destination would not be reached by the traditional route.

How can the Labour Party regain its sense of direction? My contention, in this essay, is that it cannot be done so long as politicians are content to rely on their 'hunch' and empirical experience. The Labour Party has lost its way not only because it lacks a map of the new country it is crossing, but because it thinks maps unnecessary for experienced travellers.

To-day we can see the drawbacks as well as the advantages of this stubborn empiricism. Labour policy has always been an amalgam. It consists, first, of a number of concrete proposals and, secondly, of those ethical aspirations which constitute our socialist tradition. By 1950 most of the proposals had been implemented; and the tradition had been confused by the impact of emergency after emergency upon Government policy. Are food subsidies and price controls temporary wartime expedients, to be dispensed with as soon as we can return to the price system; or are they part of the structure of a socialist State? Does democratic socialism involve the permanence of a mixed economy; and, if so, should profit-making in the private sector be encouraged or limited? Should wages be left to find their own level through collective bargaining, or is it the function of a Labour Government to modify the wages structure in the light of national interests and social justice? Is a centralised public corporation a more socialist method of running a public utility than municipal or co-operative ownership? Does socialist principle demand that we should receive our spectacles and dentures free, but pay for travelling on nationalised railways? Is there anything about a comprehensive school which makes it the chosen instrument of socialist secondary education as against a direct-grant school, where every place is allotted by competitive examination?

2

In the field of external affairs, similar questions crowd upon us. Is the object of a socialist defence policy to contain communism or to deter Russian military aggression? If it is the former, can we avoid suppressing social revolution in the colonial areas, or justify the recognition of Communist China? How can we reconcile the Labour Government's economic policy in Persia and Malaya with its avowed objective of raising the standard of living of the backward peoples? If it was right to give complete independence to India, despite the risk that she might leave the Commonwealth and even join the Russian bloc, why did we adopt the opposite policy in the Middle East? How can a socialist oppose British participation in a United Western Europe, while bowing to the American desire for a rearmed Germany?

Merely to ask these questions is to indicate the confusion which arises as soon as we seek to relate our practice to our socialist ideals. The continental Marxists certainly blunted their capacity for practical reforms by forcing their policies into conformity with a rigid doctrine. The Labour Party has gone to the other extreme. It capsulated its theory into a number of measures. Once these reforms had been accomplished, its only guide for future action was a tradition, which could be interpreted in any number of contradictory ways. The Conservatives can afford to rely on tradition and the leadership of men who are accepted as its interpreters. Indeed, conservatism can be defined as whatever the Conservative leader does or says with the consent of his party. But tradition, and the Conservative Party which is its guardian, is democracy's brake on social change. The dynamic can only be provided by a party which challenges the *status quo* on grounds of principle and uses theory to expose the inadequacy of tradition as a guide to action. We have seen, in Australia and New Zealand, what happens to labour parties which dispense with socialism. Now we ourselves are faced with a similar danger—that our socialism may degenerate into labourism. If this happens, politics will become a matter of 'ins' and 'outs'. Soon there will be no deep difference between the two parties, and the dynamic of

3

social change will be taken over by new and dangerous political movements.

II. *Pragmatism and Philosophy*

Most of the early Fabians—the one outstanding exception was George Bernard Shaw—repudiated socialist theory as dangerous Teutonic verbiage. They assumed that everyone knew the difference between justice and injustice, happiness and unhappiness, and that it was the job of the Fabian Society to show the British trade unionist—and any politician who cared to listen—the way to make Britain an efficient example of socially planned happiness. This Benthamite approach to socialism, in contrast with the Marxist theories of the Continent, had considerable advantages. It suited the anti-intellectual bias of the Labour Movement, and it faithfully reflected the conscientious objection to dogma, whether theological or political, on which our British conception of personal freedom rests. Moreover, by repudiating classical Marxism, it enabled the Labour Party, in its formative years, to welcome into its ranks all men of goodwill—the Christian Socialist, for instance, and the middle-class Liberal in search of a new vehicle of social reform—and not only the class-conscious worker. It was largely because the Party accepted this unphilosophic Fabian approach that it was able to become a national party and to assume the national responsibilities of government more easily than any Socialist Party in Europe.

It is noteworthy, however, that the Webbs, who started as the most intolerant exponents of unphilosophic Benthamism, ended as the evangelists of Soviet civilisation. Was this merely an example of senile decay? On the contrary, I believe that it was partly due to an acute apprehension of changing world conditions in the 1930's. Pragmatic social reform was sufficient so long as the balance of world power and the role of Great Britain in that balance were assumed as eternal verities. When these crumbled away, a philosophy of history became more and more necessary. The failure of the Webbs was not that they accepted this necessity in their old age, but that, trained as

4

pragmatic social scientists, they proved themselves somewhat ingenuous students of philosophy, accepting Communist theory and practice in their old age as unreflectively as they accepted Benthamism in their youth.

The Webbs were not the only socialist intellectuals who forsook pragmatism in the 1930's. R. H. Tawney, whose philosophic training was much more thorough, had long been studying Marxism and successfully assimilated its method of historical analysis into his Christian philosophy. Harold Laski, on the other hand, like the Webbs, imposed Marxism as a superstructure on his utilitarian principles, and never succeeded in moulding the two into a consistent system. John Strachey swallowed it in a single heady draught and was the only Englishman who succeeded, not merely in translating Marx, but in re-thinking his system in Anglo-Saxon terms. It is no exaggeration to say that Tawney, Laski, Strachey and the Webbs dominated the thought of young socialists in the 1930's and deeply influenced many practical politicians in the Shadow Cabinet. The Left Book Club replaced the Fabian Society as the home of the intellectual *avant-garde*.

But this victory of Marxist theory was short-lived. Communist opposition to the war in 1939 split and ultimately destroyed the Left Book Club, and the Labour victory of 1945 brought with it a return to the old-fashioned Fabian approach. Intellectuals, who had dallied with Marx and preached class war in the 1930's, now vied with each other in picturing themselves as common-sense fellows with no time for theorising. The attention which the writings of Tawney and Laski received from the Labour Cabinet hardly encouraged anyone to follow in their philosophic footsteps. Since the war, only one book has been published in Britain which even pretends to analyse the principles or the philosophy of democratic socialism.[1] Such speculations are left to the exponents of American free enterprise and Russian communism.

My contention is that this absence of a theoretical basis for practical programmes of action, is the main reason why the

[1] The Rt. Hon. P. C. Gordon Walker, *Restatement of Liberty* (Hutchinson).

post-war Labour Government marked the end of a century of social reform and not, as its socialist supporters had hoped, the beginning of a new epoch. To say this is not to condemn it. The development from the liberalism of 1906 to the modern Welfare State had to be completed; so did the transformation of the Empire into the Commonwealth. But neither of these processes was explicitly socialist. The principle of national self-determination, which Labour has fulfilled in its Indian policy and on which it is working in the Colonial Empire, is essentially liberal; and the planned Welfare State is really the adaptation of capitalism to the demands of modern trade unionism. The mixed economy, evolved in the decade between 1940 and 1950, has not abolished competitive free enterprise, but adapted it to meet the social and economic demands of organised labour. What was achieved by the first Labour Government was, in fact, the climax of a long process, in the course of which capitalism has been civilised and, to a large extent, reconciled with the principles of democracy. By refusing to accept the Marxist philosophy, we have almost succeeded in disproving its prophecies of inevitable conflict. This is a historic achievement, but the fact remains that, in achieving it, the Labour Party is in danger of becoming not the party of change, but the defender of the post-war *status quo*.

Philosophy begins where pragmatism fails. When the common-sense socialist has come to the end of his programme and there are no longer a number of obvious reforms which men of goodwill broadly agree should be carried out, it is time to sit back and reflect. How can this process of self-analysis best be begun? Certainly not by hurriedly borrowing a ready-made philosophy from elsewhere and forcing the facts of our history and the ideals of our movement into its rigid doctrines. That was the mistake of Laski and the Webbs, as well as of John Strachey in the 1930's. A sound philosophy of democratic socialism, as Evan Durbin realised in his sadly underestimated *Politics of Democratic Socialism*, must be derived from an examination of our own implicit and explicit principles of action and from a fresh appraisal of the facts of the situation.

III. *The Idea of Progress and the Fallacy of Materialism*

Let us take the principles of action first. Do we assume that, with the usual setbacks, the world is steadily progressing towards unity and freedom; and that democratic socialism, or something like it, will eventually be the pattern of a world government? Or have we lost faith in the progress which was the almost universal belief not only of the early Fabians, but of the whole civilised world at the beginning of this century?

A simple test of this is to take two extreme points of view, those of H. G. Wells and Arnold Toynbee. Wells writes,[1]

> Our history has traced a steady growth of the social and political units into which men have combined. In the brief period of ten thousand years these units have grown from the small family tribe of the early Neolithic culture to the vast united realms—vast, yet still too small and partial—of the present time. And this change in size of the state—a change manifestly incomplete—has been accompanied by profound changes in all its nature. Compulsion and servitude have given way to ideas of associated freedom, and the sovereignty that was once concentrated in an autocratic king and god has been widely diffused throughout the community.

In this passage the whole illusion of automatic progress is concisely expressed. History is the story of the evolution of society from the small unit to the large unit, and from the unit based on compulsion to the unit based on voluntary association; and this process will go on until we reach a world state, with no compulsions.

Towards the end of his life Wells began to despair, because he realised the failure of his implicit principle, that *the enlargement of scientific knowledge, i.e. power to control nature and men, necessarily increases freedom.* Faced by the obvious failure of rationalism to rationalise human nature, he moved very near to the pessimistic position of Arnold Toynbee.[2]

> Primitive societies may be likened to people lying torpid upon a ledge on a mountain-side, with a precipice below and a precipice

---

[1] P. 1142 of the fifth revised edition of *The Outline of History.*
[2] Abridged *Study of History*, (ed. Somervell) p. 49.

above; civilisations may be likened to companions of these sleepers who have just risen to their feet and have started to climb up the face of the cliff above; while we for our part may liken ourselves to observers whose field of vision is limited to the ledge and to the lower slopes of the upper precipice and who have come upon the scene at the moment when the different members of the party happen to be in these respective postures and positions. The recumbent figures, despite our first impression, cannot be paralytics in reality; for they cannot have been born on the ledge, and no human muscles except their own can have hoisted them to this halting place. On the other hand, their companions who are climbing at the moment have only just left the same ledge; and, since the next ledge is out of sight, we do not know how high or how arduous the next pitch may be. We only know that it is impossible to halt and rest.

Most of us would now agree that Toynbee's sense of direction was better than that of the early Wells. Yet until the 1930's Wells's illusions were shared by Liberals, Marxists and early Fabians; they were, indeed, the climate of all progressive public opinion.

This materialist conception of progress was based on assumptions about human behaviour which psychological research has shown to have no basis in reality, and on a theory of democratic politics which has been confuted by the facts of the last thirty years. There is neither a natural identity of interests nor yet an inherent contradiction in the economic system. The growth of science and popular education does not automatically produce an 'upward' evolution in society, if by 'upward' is meant from servile to democratic forms; and the apocalyptic assumption that, after a period of dictatorship, a proletarian revolution must achieve a free and equal society is equally invalid. *The evolutionary and the revolutionary philosophies of progress have both proved false.* Judging by the facts, there is far more to be said for the Christian doctrine of original sin than for Rousseau's fantasy of the noble savage, or Marx's vision of the classless society.

Our first task, therefore, is to re-define progress. In what sense can we speak of it at all? Is there, as every communist, as well as every liberal and socialist, has believed, any upward movement in human history, or is it merely a story without plot or meaning?

To begin with, we must accept the fact that, in the strictest sense of the words, there is no such thing as moral progress. For morality consists in the decision to do good, and there is no evidence that more men decide more often to do what they believe to be their duty in a civilised society than do so in a primitive society. From the aspect of *individual* morality, modern civilisation merely faces men with different choices from those presented at earlier stages of our history. It enlarges the area of free choice. It enables us to cure sickness on a huge scale—and to destroy each other on a huge scale. It enables us to liberate each other on a huge scale—and to tyrannise each other on a huge scale. Men do, of course, 'behave better' to each other in a society which forbids slavery than in one which tolerates it. But, in terms of individual morality, there are just as many opportunites for a slave-owner to be a saint as for a citizen of a free democracy. Civilisation does not *make* us morally better, any more than democracy *makes* us use our liberty. The only continuous lines which we can trace in human history—and even these sag sometimes for hundreds of years at a time—are (i) the social accumulation of knowledge, and (ii) the enlargement, through this accumulation, of men's power to control both nature and one another.

But both these lines of progress are morally neutral. The individual and the society that possess more knowledge and power are not necessarily better than their backward ancestors. Here is one point where Toynbee's picture is more acceptable that that of Wells or Marx—its rejection of any moral determinism in history. There is no automatic progress or improvement in human nature, but there is an almost automatic accumulation of knowledge and power, which we can use equally for self-destruction or for self-emancipation.

Of course, it would be absurd to deny the existence in history of periods of *social* progress. Athenian democracy was

9

an advance on the Solonian system, just as our own Welfare State is an improvement on the social morality of the 1840's. *The socialist measures this progress of social morality by the degree of equality and respect for individual personality expressed in the distribution of power and in the institutions of law and property within a state. This standard indeed, is what we mean by the socialist ideal.*

It is important to observe, however, that there is no evidence of any continuous upward line of social progress. Free societies, in the sense we have given to the word, have existed at various times in recorded history and probably in prehistory as well. They have grown and they have perished, to be replaced by despotism and exploitation. Once we understand the nature of human freedom, this will not seem surprising, nor will it depress us unduly. For the social accumulation of knowledge and power does not make it any *easier* for men to build a free society. Knowledge can be used to enslave much more easily than to liberate; and destruction is as natural to man as construction. T. H. Huxley was right when, in a famous essay, he compared a free society to a garden. Nature produces either a wilderness of weeds or an arid patch of ground. Left to itself, a garden runs wild, and the gardener spends far more time in rooting out weeds than in planting flowers. Social morality, freedom and equality do not grow by any law of economics or politics, but only with the most careful cultivation. So far, therefore, from viewing history as a steady advance towards freedom, we should regard exploitation and slavery as the normal state of man and view the brief epochs of liberty as tremendous achievements. They could only be preserved for a few generations by constant cultivation and they cannot be expected to become the general rule.

This is the point of departure for a modern theory of socialism. Instead of regarding social change as tending towards the enlargement of freedom, we must assume that increased concentration of power, whether in the form of technological development or social organisation, will always produce exploitation, injustice and inequality in a society, unless the community possesses a social conscience strong enough to civilize them. Human institutions will always be not merely amoral but immoral, as Reinhold Niebuhr showed in his famous book, unless they are moralised by individual men and women aware of this proclivity and waging unceasing war against it. Every economic system, whether capitalist or socialist, degenerates into a system of privilege and exploitation unless it is policed by a social morality, which can only reside in a minority of citizens. Every political party degenerates into office-seeking, unless its leaders are faced by an opposition within the ranks. Every Church becomes a vested interest without its heretics, and every political system, including democracy, ossifies into an oligarchy. Freedom is always in danger, and the majority of mankind will always acquiesce in its loss, unless a minority is willing to challenge the privileges of the few and the apathy of the masses.

In the nineteenth century this challenge was the task of liberalism. To-day it has fallen to socialism. But we cannot fulfil it so long as we base our policy on the materialist fallacy that material progress *makes* men either free or equal. One particularly vicious form of this fallacy is the belief that economics are the determinant factors in social change and that, if we achieve economic justice, we automatically secure human freedom.

Unfortunately, man moulds not only nature to his use, but also his fellow men: if he is a tool-using animal, as Marx declared, one of the handiest tools is his neighbour. The school, the press, the radio, the party machine, the army, the factory, are all instruments through which man, unless checked by a social conscience armed with sanctions, will exert power over the minds of his fellow men. The Political Revolution, which has concentrated coercive power and thought-control in a few hands, is just as important a historical fact as the Industrial Revolution. Yet since Graham Wallas, almost nothing has been written by socialists about the Political Revolution, although it was the techniques of thought-control and centralised coercion which frustrated the apocalyptic visions of liberals and Marxists and made possible both the modern Western democracy and the totalitarian state. Without these, it might have been possible, as the Liberals hoped, for the nation state to wither away into economic brotherhood of man, or for the Leninist dictatorship of the proletariat to develop into a peaceful anarchy, in which coercive authority was scarcely apparent. But actually those who control the media of mass communication and the means of destruction (propaganda and the armed forces) are far more powerful to-day than the owners of the means of production. The state is no longer the executive committee of the bourgeoisie: the bourgeoisie are becoming the managers working for the state.

Marx saw that, though capitalism was the enemy, the Industrial Revolution was 'objectively progressive,' a stage in social development. Yet, as soon as capitalism reached maturity, it became a system of privilege and exploitation. To-day the enemy of human freedom is the managerial society and the central coercive power which goes with it. And yet the Political Revolution has been 'objectively progressive', in the sense that the instruments of mass communication and coercion, if restrained by social morality, *can* be used to enlarge freedom. Just as capitalism *could* be civilised into the Welfare State, so the managerial society *can* be civilised into democratic socialism.

The Soviet Union is the most extreme example of managerialism, because its Stalinist rulers consciously repudiate the primacy of morality over expediency, and so destroy the possibility of an active social conscience, which could save them from the corruption of power. The capitalist class never did that, and this is why capitalist development did not fulfil the prophecies of Marx. No capitalist country was ever so theoretically and methodically capitalist as Russia is Stalinite to-day. This is also the reason why, judged by European standards, the U.S.A. is a better form of society than the U.S.S.R. In America, a liberal and Christian morality, and a Constitution and political tradition derived from it, have frustrated the full development of capitalism and still put up strong resistance against totalitarian tendencies. To reject America as a capitalist country and to treat the Soviet Empire as an example of socialist planning is to make nonsense of every one of our ideals. In reality, they are the two great examples of the modern managerial state, the one consciously and systematically managerial, the other moving towards the same end under the pressure of the Cold War. But whereas, in the U.S.A., totalitarianism and aggressiveness can still be checked by social conscience, in Russia they cannot. We can co-operate with the Americans as allies, influencing their policies despite their superior strength. It would be folly to expect such a relationship with the Soviet Union. Co-existence, yes. Mutually beneficial agreements, yes. But never co-operation.

One factor which has prevented many British socialists from accepting this obvious fact is the belief that in some sense the Soviet Union is a 'workers' state'. In fact, like all totalitarian states, it is an elite society, created by a revolutionary intelligentsia, which admittedly merely used the working-class movement, such as it was, in order to engineer its own capture of power. Indeed, the appeal of the communist philosophy, as distinct from communist slogans, has always been to the disillusioned intelligentsia. It offers them the power of which they are deprived, and a theory to justify its ruthless use; and it provides them with a scientific philosophy which satisfies their religious cravings while permitting them to feel modern and up-to-date.

It is noteworthy that the chief successes of communism since the Russian Revolution have been in backward countries, where popular education scarcely exists and a genuine working-class movement has for that reason failed to develop. In such countries democracy must be a sham, since power is held in a few hands and public opinion consists of a few thousand people. *The carriers of communism in Asia are a tiny, educated minority, who form the social conscience and who have been personally wounded by the insolence of Western imperialism and white ascendancy*. The coolie in Malaya, or for that matter the tribesman in Nigeria, does not want *either* liberty, equality and fraternity, *or* the dictatorship of the proletariat. He is below the level of such political aspirations. Not so the minor civil servant, the university professor and the lawyer. The affronts perpetrated by the white man on this social conscience are a far more important communist lever than the economic condition of the masses.[1] Communism enlists the conscience and idealism of this elite and offers it a 'career open to the talents' in its totalitarian society. In the twentieth-century democracy is no longer, as it was in the period of Marx, a *necessary* stage on the way to industrialisation. Unless trained in the Western tradition, as the Indians were, the elite does not desire it: and the masses do not require it, since they can be modernised (taught to drive tractors, fly aeroplanes and worship Stalin) without any democratic liberation. For fighting a modern war, for working on a collective farm, or for repetition work in a factory, the Chinese coolie is more malleable material and more expendable than a Western European worker, or a New England farmer. So too, the colonial intelligentsia are more suitable members of a communist managerial class than Westerners, imbued with democratic traditions. Totalitarianism may well be the normal state of twentieth-century man, unless he has the good fortune to belong to a society which was either modernised before the century began, or indoctrinated with Western standards by a colonial power.

The recognition that progress does not necessarily bring freedom has led a considerable number of socialist intellectuals to accept defeat and to withdraw from politics into mysticism or quietism. But this is not the only conclusion which can be drawn. Facing the century of totalitarianism, we can choose between two philosophies, symbolised by the figures of Buddha and Prometheus. Buddha represents the withdrawal from the struggle for freedom. For the Oriental Buddhist or for the Western defeatist, intellectual humility is the greatest virtue; the good man is not involved, but detached; he accepts this world as a vale of woe and seeks realisation in a transcendental

---

[1] The success of the Labour Party's Indian policy confirms this view. It brought no economic benefit to the masses. But it has cured the anti-British resentment of the educated minority, which detests racial inequality and demands power and status for itself.

eternity. The other philosophy, that of the sceptical humanist, is symbolised by Prometheus, chained to his Caucasian peak, with the eagle pecking out his liver. Prometheus stole fire from the gods in order to help his fellow men. He did not believe that any law of nature or divine purpose would automatically give freedom and happiness to his fellow men. Neither God nor history was on his side. It was his duty to steal fire, in defiance of law and order, and to prefer eternal agony to the denial of truth. He was surrounded by mysteries, but he recognised that they were veils to be pierced, not divine realities to be worshipped. So too the humanist to-day knows that we are surrounded by misery and injustice, and that it is quite possible that all we have achieved in Western Europe may be destroyed. But he also knows that it is man's destiny to struggle against this natural process, and that there is no more justification for pessimism in politics than there is for a gardener to say, 'I'll give up weeding because it's a wet summer.'

By rejecting the automatism of Wells and Marx and the defeatism of Koestler or Aldous Huxley, we purify our socialist philosophy of illusions, which for many years have been sapping its strength. To realise that the socialist society is not the norm, evolved by material conditions, but the exception, imposed on immoral society by human will and social conscience, is not to emasculate our socialism, but to set ourselves a challenge.

Moreover, it shows us another difference between socialism and communism. The communist, like the Calvinist, derives his self-confidence from the sense that history is on his side and that his victory is predestined by forces largely outside his control. The democratic socialist draws his inspiration from the belief that nothing but human will and social conscience can liberate men from a historical process which, if left to itself, leads to slavery, exploitation and war. The test of communism is the statistical success of each Five Year Plan, and the size and strength of the Russian Empire. The test of socialism is the extent to which it shapes a people's institutions to the moral standards of freedom—even at the cost of a lower standard of living or the surrender of an empire.

IV. *The Century of Totalitarianism*

With this background, let us look at our present prospects. Many socialists assume that a third world war would 'destroy civilisation'. There is no evidence for this, though it would be quite likely to destroy Europe. The fact is that two world wars have not only accelerated scientific advance, but enlarged the *possibilities* of human liberation. In the Western world, the concept of welfare economics, for instance, was largely a product of wartime exigencies. If the twentieth century had brought a long period of peace, the Western democracies would not have accepted all those responsibilities which the governments found necessary to assume in total war. The National Health Service is a by-product of the blitz; the enormous improvement in the status of the American Negro is a by-product of war mobilisation. Total war and preparation for total war, do of course, distort peacetime economies, but they may also drive towards the reluctant acceptance of fair shares and equality of opportunity as practical principles of political and industrial organisation. Despite all the pessimists, there has been an astonishing process of liberation inside the Atlantic democracies during the last forty years.

Outside the Atlantic area, the liberating effect of two world wars is still more marked. The first produced the October Revolution in Russia, the second the national and social uprising of the Far Eastern peoples. We, of course, tend to see only the threat to European civilisation which they present. But, in the perspective of the next fifty years, this is likely to look as jaundiced as Burke's view of the French Revolution. Then too, on the side of the Revolution, liberation and imperialism were inextricably bound together; in the anti-revolutionary camp the defence of established liberties was equally hopelessly involved with dynastic reaction. Social evolution was the result not of the unconditional surrender of one side to the other, but of a drawn battle. The position in the 1950's is in this respect similar. A new world order and world balance of power is in process of long-drawn-out establishment. Even if the Atlantic powers were to win an outright victory in war, they could not destroy communism, any more than the anti-Napoleonic coalition destroyed the French Revolution. Nor can the Russians destroy democracy, since a Stalinite world state, ruled from the Kremlin, would ultimately be overthrown by the national and social forces it released in climbing to power. The socialist, therefore, while prepared to join the Atlantic alliance in order to defend himself against the present threat of Soviet imperialism to Europe, must accept both intellectually and emotionally the fact that communism outside Europe is still a liberative force. He must face and overcome an acute dilemma. The throwing off of European ascendancy, however brutal the forms it takes, is a necessary phase of Asiatic and African liberation: yet, whenever the revolution is captured by the Stalinites they threaten the colonial peoples with a new imperialism, which concentrates power more terribly than its predecessor.

Let us put the same dilemma in economic terms. The whole history of Europe since the Reformation indicates that the establishment of the nation state and large-scale industrialisation are the two social techniques for liberating the masses from localised enslavement to the soil and to nature. In Europe and North America, this was achieved by the bourgeois revolution. Outside this limited area, and in this present century, the social conditions for a bourgeois revolution are not present, and this is why, in the absence of any alternative instrument of modernisation, communism often becomes the chosen instrument of history.

There was, of course, one other instrument available, but European liberalism and socialism blunted its edge. As the Webbs saw when, in their early years, they were imperialist anti-Boers, it would have been possible for the European powers to carry through the industrialisation of, say, the Middle East or India. If there had been no democratic and socialist movements protesting against imperialism, it would theoretically have been possible to imagine the ruthless economic reconstruction of Middle Eastern or Indian life under white rule and capitalist exploitation. The Germans might have created an imperial welfare state, with Slavs and Russians as second-rate citizens; and the British an Indian and African empire of the same sort; and it might all have lasted for a hundred or five hundred years. In these capitalist Empires, the destruction of peasant proprietorship and the substitution of the large-scale agricultural unit (not as a collective, but as an East-Elbian estate on an enormous scale) might have produced the sort of managerial society foreseen in Jack London's *Iron Heel*.

Finally, no doubt, white imperialism would have been destroyed by its inherent contradictions and by a classical Marxist revolution of the coloured proletariat against their European rulers. Indeed, what I have done in these paragraphs is merely to restate the Marxist-Leninist vision of how world history would develop. But all this did not happen. Instead, the economic basis of European ascendancy was destroyed by two world wars, and American capitalism, which has succeeded to world leadership, is most unlikely to assume the role of nineteenth-century Britain. The U.S.A. is a relatively self-sufficient economy, with an isolationist tradition; and American capitalism, after its inter-war experiences in Germany and elsewhere, has shown no inclination to undertake large-scale overseas investment. American imperialism, if it develops, will be strategically motivated.

The disintegration of the economic basis of European imperialism was accompanied by a moral disintegration as well. After 1918 Western man lost his faith in the White Man's Burden. For a generation liberals and socialists had been campaigning against the evils of imperialism. Now their ideas infected the ruling class and destroyed its own confidence in itself. Owing to its peculiar development, the U.S.A. had always been opposed to colonial empires. Now, President Wilson's naïve theory of national self-determination was accepted, in Europe as well, as the democratic solution of all political problems, including that of the relationship between the white and the colonial peoples. Far too easily, it was assumed that the march of human progress would be resumed if each oppressed people were permitted to establish its own nation state and to institute parliamentary democracy on the Western pattern.

Unfortunately there were no grounds for this assumption. Even in Western Europe, the destruction of feudalism did not take place under the forms of representative government. In the very few countries where it operates successfully, parliamentary democracy is the latest phase of a long process, which has taken place for the most part under autocratic governmental forms. Democracy, indeed, is a sophisticated and subtle form of government, which except in countries with established civil liberties and a high degree of political education, will be manipulated by the ruling groups to retard social change. It is unsuited, therefore, to societies which require to be rapidly industrialised against the opposition of the ruling oligarchy and of the illiterate masses. Wherever Western imperialism is replaced by this kind of pseudo-democracy, there is a danger that sooner or later Communism will take over the social revolution. For a centralised, one-party state, with a clear-cut, if mechanical, programme of modernisation, is better adapted to the requirements of a backward people than a spurious imitation of the British or American Constitution, combined with a reactionary social system. It was the understanding of this which led the Webbs to move from their support for imperialism in 1900 to their acceptance of communism in 1932.

Once again it is useful to compare our twentieth-century crisis with that of the French Revolutionary wars. Burke and Paine both tried to prove that there was a simple conflict of right and wrong; on one side stood freedom, on the other tyranny, and everyone was morally bound to make up his mind and work for the victory of the good.

We can now see that Burke and Paine were wrong. War and revolution can never provide us with simple moral issues. The defender of law and order defends privilege as well; and the revolutionary, in his attack on antiquated social forms, threatens a settled pattern of rights and liberties. The dynamic of social change is always tyrannical and usually ends by becoming imperialist: and, under the impact of revolutionary imperialism, the defenders of liberty are driven to support counter-revolution.

Those who believe that the task of socialism is to discover a dynamic which can challenge the dynamic of communism are therefore neglecting the clear lesson of history. If we construct an anti-communist ideology, or take part in organising an anti-Cominform, we shall merely intensify the Cold War and confirm the illusion that the preservation of freedom requires the defeat of communism. In fact, if freedom is to survive, it is essential that neither the U.S.A. nor the Soviet Union should win, and that ideological passion should subside. What the Western socialist needs to-day is not a crusading creed, but a critical attitude to both ideologies; and the role of the British Labour Movement is to furnish an example of this critical humanism in action. Sceptical, but not cynical; detatched, but not neutral; rational, but not dogmatically rationalist. The Promethean social conscience, which I have described on an earlier page, is the only force which can prevent the modern state from degenerating into a managerial society, or the East-West conflict into World War III. It exists everywhere where scientific method and critical analysis are taught (and this includes the Soviet Union as well as the U.S.A.). But in most of the world it can merely act as a brake on totalitarian forces. Only in post-imperial Western Europe, and particularly in this country, could it mould the policies of a nation.

V. Socialism and the Colonial Peoples

Let me illustrate this critical spirit in relation to the central issue of the Cold War. We have seen that, although the Soviet Union is the supreme example of the totalitarian state, communism presents itself to many colonial peoples as a liberative force, and democracy as the defence of a corrupt oligarchy.

What should the socialist do in face of this dilemma? Should he put his trust in plans for world mutual aid, and seek to persuade the Americans that the only way to fight communism effectively is to provide dollars and technical assistance in order to raise the living standards of the backward territories?

The ideal is a noble one; and, if the Americans divert some of the resources, at present concentrated on rearmament, to its achievement, the danger of world war would be substantially reduced. For it is the unmeasured concentration on rearmament which is distorting all the Western economies and gradually creating a situation where we must either make war or collapse. To persuade the Americans, therefore, to give mutual aid a high priority would be a victory for restraint and sanity.

But it is important not to claim more for mutual aid than it can achieve and, in particular, not to fall into the materialist fallacy of assuming that economics provide the prime motive of political action. The dynamic of social revolution in Asia and Africa is not a mass demand for tractors or for bread, but the will and the social conscience of a small intelligentsia, whose aim (national liberation and modernisation) is shared neither by the ruling oligarchy nor by the masses. As we know well from our own history, a revolution is not willed by 'the people', but by a new social force with a new philosophy.

Mutual aid, therefore, even when it is combined with democracy, will not necessarily provide an antidote to communist revolutions. Parliamentary institutions retard social change by deliberately ensuring that it does not greatly injure minority groups or outpace the natural conservatism of the masses. This is why they work successfully only after civil liberties and a sound administration have been firmly established and the masses liberated, usually by undemocratic means. To impose modern democracy on a feudal or primitive social structure, therefore, merely provides the ruling groups with an instrument for preserving their privileges.

This is what has happened throughout the Middle East, as well as in, for instance, the Philippines and South Korea. In all these countries, the forms of democracy are being used to prevent popular emancipation, just as they were in the Balkan states before the war.

Economic and technical assistance provided to such

'democracies' will either be wasted or aggravate the social conflict. In any event, the new elites, which are the carriers of communism, will certainly regard it as an attempt to bolster up counter-revolution, and very often this is what it in fact will be.

The position is aggravated when the Western Powers find it necessary to keep troops in such 'democracies', or to exploit the raw materials which are usually their only source of wealth. Then both national and social aspirations are canalised against the West; Russia is regarded as a rival great power whose good offices can be used to get rid of the foreigner in present occupation; and even the ruling oligarchy has to talk nationalism in order to avert attention from the social crisis. This is the situation with which we are familiar in Egypt and Persia.

The socialist, therefore, who regards (i) the granting of national independence, (ii) the encouragement of parliamentary democracy, and (iii) the provision of economic aid as the complete socialist answer to communism is glossing over the real difficulty which faces us. Even if the U.S.A. (which is most unlikely) provided sufficient resources for a world-wide attack on low living standards, the result in many countries would not be to contain communism, but to create more favourable conditions for social revolution. We should still, therefore, be faced with the problem what to do when a revolutionary dictatorship, almost certainly with Russian assistance, seizes power in a backward country which we are seeking to modernise under Western patronage. Should the revolution be crushed, as the French tried to crush it in Indo-China, or tolerated, as the Labour Government tolerated the Chinese Communists? And if we recognise successful revolutions—and even assist them when they quarrel with the Kremlin—why do we continue to assert that we share the American objective of containing communism throughout the world? Here is an unresolved contradiction, which inhibits any clear formulation of socialist policy.

We can see this contradiction in its sharpest form by examining two contrasting pairs of countries, Yugoslavia and Greece, and Turkey and Persia. In Greece, at tremendous cost, the social revolution was crushed and vast amounts of economic aid were provided to support an ineffective and corrupt parliamentary democracy. In Yugoslavia, the social revolution was pushed through under Russian control. Now that Tito has broken with the Kremlin, there at last exists an example of national communism. Who can honestly assert that there is more hope of the enlargement of freedom in democratic Greece than in communist Yugoslavia? Or who would claim that Yugoslavia would have been the better for an Anglo-American occupation in 1945 and the restoration of democracy under King Peter?

The comparison of Turkey and Persia is equally instructive. In the former, Kemal Ataturk with the benevolent assistance of the Soviet Union, led a revolutionary war of liberation *against* Britain and the Greeks, and then instituted a dictatorship in order to modernise the country. Persia, on the other hand, like the rest of the Middle East, is ruled by a Parliament controlled by an oligarchy. The revolutionary Tudeh Party was suppressed, with British and American encouragement, and attempts were made to do a deal with the oligarchy, with the object of retaining British control of oil production. The result of this policy was to make nonsense of Mr. Bevin's claim that his aim was to raise the standard of living of the poor fellaheen. Turkey can be friendly to us (as Israel can) because she has won her revolutionary war of independence. Persia, Iraq and Egypt cannot. They seethe with suppressed revolution and overt xenophobia. Is it not the lesson of the Labour Government's failure in the Middle East that it may be less dangerous to permit revolution and dictatorship (even when their motive force is hatred of ourselves) than to defend our strategic and commercial interest by a combination of military force and political fraud? The socialist must remain sceptical of plans for combating communism which really involve the suppression of national and social revolution among the colonial peoples. In the history of every Western democracy, the revolutionary war or civil war has been the first act of nationhood, just as the revolutionary army has been the first instrument of national unification and popular education. These are historical facts which the Russian Marxists have carefully studied, and from which they have drawn important conclusions. It is time that we studied them too and learnt from the French experience in Indo-China that the spread of communism may be a lesser evil than the containment of it by a ruinous colonial war.

But it is by no means certain that every social revolution will be taken over by the Kremlin, if its leaders are left free to make their own policy. Since the war Indonesia and Burma chose independence and suppressed their Communist Parties; and Tito quarrelled with the Kremlin. If the Tudeh Party in Persia, Viet-Minh in Indo-China and Mao Tse-tung are now allies of Russia, it must be admitted that Western policy did nothing to dissuade them. Social revolution in a backward country always begins as an alliance of very varied elements, among which the Stalinites are rarely the most important. Whether the Communists come to dominate the revolution depends at least as much on Western policy as on the activities of the Kremlin. Only too often strategic and economic policies, designed to contain communism, have in fact, by supporting counter-revolution, played into the hands of the Soviet Union. Just as the Cold War is driving the Soviet Union to adopt more and more brutal methods within its Empire, so it is pushing the Western democracies into a half-hearted attempt to revert to imperialist methods, which drive the social conscience of the colonial peoples into slavery to totalitarianism. The American isolationist, who reacts so violently against the gigantic bill for rearmament and foreign aid, is nearer the tradition of Americanism than the New Deal prophets of America's world-wide responsibilities. In the past, the outstanding virtue of American democracy has been its anti-colonial bias. Instead of seeking to encourage the Americans to overcome this bias and underwrite our imperial commitments, we should influence them to revert to the moderate policies of the period of Marshall Aid, to limit their arms programme to what they can sustain for at least a generation, and to take the risk in Asia and Africa of leaving unfilled the 'political vacuum' left by the dismantling of the old European empires. An unfilled vacuum is sometimes less dangerous than the frustration of social revolution in the name of democracy.

VI. Conclusions: Domestic Policy

It is now time to return to the question with which we started. The Labour Party, we observed, lost its sense of direction before the 1950 Election. Can we use the world picture we have sketched in order to rediscover our bearings? We are certainly not in a position as yet to map the new route to socialism. That will require (i) a detailed assessment of the balance of world power, and in particular, of those internal forces which mould the external policies of the U.S.A. and the Soviet Union, and so determine the course of the Cold War; (ii) an analysis of our strength, as measured against our commitments in a world where colonial emancipation, combined with population pressure, has turned the terms of trade permanently against us; and (iii) a fresh investigation of the changes in the internal structure of the country since 1940. These vital pieces of research have yet to be undertaken. Meanwhile, the best we can hope to do is to ask the relevant questions, which must be answered before the second stage of socialism can be worked out. The first signpost is one that is already behind us, established by the Labour Government. Although the welfare capitalism developed since 1945 is highly unstable, what *is* inviolable is the change in social climate, a change equal in importance with the liberal revolutions of 1832 and 1906. Its essence can be summed up in two principles. The first states that it is the responsibility of the democratic state to provide for every citizen, as of right, security against unemployment, sickness and old age. The second runs that it is the function of the state to plan the use of our national resources so as to maintain work for all and ensure fair shares of the national income between different sections of the community.

Of course, there are still many who still believe that these two principles should never have been conceded, since their full implementation must lead either to the collapse of our economy or to complete socialisation. The Conservative Party for instance, accepts them with the proviso that nothing must be done which undermines the incentives of free enterprise—that is to say, it accepts them in theory, but not in practice. But the fact remains that the social climate—and with it the categories of political controversy—was changed decisively when the Labour Government succeeded in preserving, *after the war had ended*, the full employment, the system of redistributive taxation, and the central planning of the economy which had previously been regarded as temporary wartime expedients.

In working out the programme for the second stage of socialism, we must start from this change of social climate. The true aim of the Labour Movement has always been not the dramatic capture of power by the working class, but the conversion of the nation to the socialist pattern of rights and values; not the violent destruction of one economic system and the substitution of another, but the voluntary acceptance of the need for socialism in order to implement in social life the values which each citizen accepts in his personal relations. Sceptical of the Marxist doctrine of inherent conflict, the Labour Party has tenaciously assumed that British people can be persuaded by an act of collective conscience to subject economic power to public authority and to civilise the conflict inherent in social change.

This belief was vindicated in the first post-war months. At that time the British people was ready to accept the peaceful socialist revolution; and if what it got was merely welfare capitalism, the fault lay with the politicians and not with the public.

Let us define precisely where welfare capitalism falls short of socialism. Under welfare capitalism: (i) Though the national income is rather more fairly distributed than before, the concentration of capital and so of economic privilege remains unchanged. (ii) Profits, wages and salaries are still determined not by any conditions of national interest or social justice, but

26

by the traditional methods of *laisser-faire*. Under conditions of full employment, this must result in a continuous inflationary pressure, which undermines the real value of social security and small savings, as well as making our products less competitive in foreign markets and so jeopardising our capacity to maintain the standard of living. (iii) Though certain basic industries are transformed into public corporations and private industry is subject to some control, effective power remains in the hands of a small managerial and Civil Service elite.

There can be no advance to socialism unless each of these three problems is honestly faced. Can an unhealthy concentration of capital be prevented without a much greater extension of public ownership or, alternatively, a capital levy? Can inflation be countered, under conditions of full employment, without a national profits and wages policy? If not, how can such a policy be put into execution without some amendment by the trade unions of their cherished freedom of collective bargaining? Both these issues were avoided during the six years of Labour Government. They can be avoided no longer if the Labour Party is to face the future once again with a programme as challenging as that of 1945.

But, overshadowing these two questions is the threat of the managerial society. The planned economy and the centralisation of power are no longer socialist objectives. They are developing all over the world as the result of the Political Revolution, and the process is accelerated by the prevalence of war economy. The main task of socialism to-day is to prevent the concentration of power in the hands of *either* industrial management *or* the state bureaucracy—in brief, to distribute responsibility and so to enlarge freedom of choice.

This task was not even begun by the Labour Government. On the contrary, in the nationalised industries old managements were preserved almost untouched, and appointments to the national, regional and consultative boards were made as if with the express intention of affirming that no change was intended. The Government's attitude to central planning was similar. Up to 1947, no serious attempt was made to construct

even a central mechanism for assessing resources and requirements of wealth and labour, and allocating them to the various
needs. Not until the convertibility crisis was Sir Stafford Cripps
given the task of grappling with the problem, educating the
people about its nature, and developing the institutions
necessary for its solution. But even then the Government seemed
to have regarded his austerity planning as an emergency
measure, rather than as the first step towards bringing economic
power under democratic control. Just as it failed to socialise
the management of the nationalised industries, so it left the
central control of planning in the hands of an unreformed
Civil Service.

Nor was any effort made to encourage popular participation
in the new Welfare State. The Labour Movement grew up as a
working-class democracy in action. Before 1945, for hundreds
of thousands of active trade unionists and Party workers,
socialism was a way of life and a vocation. In order to counter
the danger of managerialism, it was essential to harness this
volunteer energy to the work of social transformation and so to
retain for the Party in office the dynamic of Opposition. In the
new social climate, there were endless tasks which trade
unionists, both locally and nationally, would have been ready
to undertake. They were left to infer that collective bargaining,
such as they had developed in the capitalist free-for-all, and
the humdrum job of Party organisation, were all that was
required of them. Municipal socialists—with some of their
best enterprises taken over by public corporations—were
given no vision of new socialist responsibilities. The Co-
operative Movement was not summoned to help in tackling the
problems of distribution. Instead, the impression was given
that socialism was an affair for the Cabinet, acting through the
existing Civil Service. The rest of the nation was to carry on as
before, while benefits were bestowed from above upon some,
and taken from others. Thus the first stage of socialism was
executed primarily by anti-socialist managers and neutral
Civil Servants.

We are a nation deeply imbued with a sense of social status

and inhibited by an oligarchic tradition, which makes responsibility the privilege of the educated minority and irresponsibility the negative freedom of the half-educated masses. At present the educational system, the parties and the trade union machines, instead of acting as a social solvent, are accentuating the segregation of elites. The leaders—and this applies at least as much in the Labour Movement as outside it—profoundly distrust active democracy.

Yet whether the next stage in our journey is towards socialism or a veiled form of totalitarianism largely depends on how far the state and industry are run by segregated elites, with the rest of the people passive executants of their orders. This applies to public as well as to private industry, to the trade union and Party hierarchies as well as to business concerns. In a world organised in ever larger and more inhuman units, the task of socialism is to prevent managerial responsibility degenerating into privilege. This can only be achieved by increasing, even at the cost of 'efficiency', the citizen's right to participate in the control not only of government and industry, but of the party for which he votes, and of the trade union whose card he carries. After all, it is not the pursuit of happiness but the enlargement of freedom which is socialism's highest aim.

VII. Conclusions: External Relations

When we turn from home affairs to world politics, we must finally discard the idea that British Socialism can be 'an economically closed system'.[1] This kind of isolationism is at least theoretically possible for the U.S.A. and the Soviet Union. For Britain it is an absurdity. Our standard of living and our survival as a nation will always be dependent on the interplay of world

---

[1] See *The Socialist Case*, by Douglas Jay (revised and republished in 1946). In his Introduction, Mr. Jay writes: 'For the purpose of clarity, the existence of international exchange is ignored, except where it is for some special reason relevant to the argument. Normally it is simpler and clearer to pursue the socialist inquiry on the assumption of an economically closed system, such as the world as a whole.'

forces, of which we are not the masters. We can neither opt out
of the Cold War, nor, so long as it continues, cut loose from
the Atlantic alliance, to which we are committed not by ideology
but by facts of geography, strategy and economics. The degree
of our political independence, therefore, will always depend
on our skill in influencing our allies, just as the degree of our
economic independence will derive from our ability to adapt
our production to changing world demands. However distaste-
ful it may be to a nation which was once the subject of world
politics, we are now one of its objects: and our survival depends
not on imperial self-assertion, but on our powers of adaptation
to an environment in process of rapid change.

This adaptation demands that we should see ourselves not as
we should like to be, but as others see us. If we pretend to
being equal partners with the U.S.A., we assume commitments
beyond our strength and so fall into an even greater degree of
dependence. If, deluding ourselves that the Commonwealth is
an independent power bloc, we stand aloof from Europe, we
forfeit the leadership of Europe, which could be ours. If we
cling too greedily to the profits of economic imperialism, we
lose the trade we could retain on terms of equality. To maintain the reality of independence we must discard some of its
fictions; to achieve greatness at our new level, we must forgo
the postures of grandeur. We can exert a decisive *influence* on
world politics once we accept the fact that we have ceased to be
a *world power* in our own right.

One of the failings of Mr. Bevin was that he never measured
our strength against our commitments and so failed to see that
we must cut our external relations according to the cloth available. In the Far East he conceded to the new realities; in the
Middle East he stubbornly resisted them; while, in his relations
with the U.S.A. and Europe, he sought to maintain a
power status far beyond our capacity. Finally, having man-
fully dispensed with American Aid in the spring of 1950, we
accepted a burden of rearmament twelve months later which
could only be sustained either with the sacrifice of the Welfare
State or by taking American Aid on American terms. The

patchwork character of this policy is only explicable on the assumption that the Cabinet never undertook a radical re-assessment of Britain's role in the post-war world. That re-assessment must be carried through before Labour is ready for another term of office.

The revolution through which the world is passing has already ended the period of European ascendancy and substituted for a European balance of power a two-world system of politics, with its capitals in Washington and Moscow. Simultaneously, the self-emancipation of the colonial peoples is undermining the traditional relationship between the highly industrialised white democracies and the producers of primary raw materials. Moreover, the overwhelming preponderance of American economic strength, now aggravated by rearmament, has destroyed any economic balance which previously existed within the non-Communist world. In these conditions it is self-deception to believe that the living standards and security enjoyed by the British people after 1945 were a *stable* achievement of socialism. Living in an age not of steady progress towards a world welfare capitalism, but of world revolution, it is folly for us to assume that the socialist's task is to assist in the gradual improvement of the material lot of the human race and the gradual enlargement of the area of human freedom. The forces of history are all pressing towards totalitarianism: in the Russian bloc, owing to the conscious policy of the Kremlin; in the free world, owing to the growth of the managerial society, the effects of total rearmament, and the repression of colonial aspirations. The task of socialism is neither to accelerate this Political Revolution, nor to oppose it (this would be as futile as opposition to the Industrial Revolution a hundred years ago), but to civilise it.

To do this we must realise that a victory for either side would be a defeat for socialism. We are members of the Atlantic alliance; but this does not mean that we are enemies of every communist revolution. We are opposed to Russian expansion, but also to an American victory. Our object is to keep the Cold War cold and, in particular, so to restrain rearmament that it remains at a level which both sides can sustain over a period of years. If this object could be achieved, there is no inherent reason why the power conflict between the two great blocs should not gradually exhaust itself during the next twenty years. The success we seek is a balance of world power, and in that balance the restraining influence of a communist China on Russia may be as vital as that of a socialist Britain on the U.S.A. If neutralism is a blind alley, ideological detachment is a requisite for those on both sides of the Iron Curtain who are seeking to strengthen the social conscience in its struggle against totalitarianism.

In the last place, we must realise that the Cold War brings possibilities of good as well as evil. Under its stress, both communists and anti-communists are overcoming antiquated forms of national sovereignty, developing new institutions of international economic planning, and accelerating the pace of social and technological change. As soon as rearmament is given an absolute priority by either side, the value of these changes is outweighed by the added risk of war and the distortion of the economy. But, while facing this danger frankly, we should not overlook the fact that the interacting pressure of Cold War (provided it can be restrained within limits) *can* create material conditions for the enlargement of freedom. The task of a socialist foreign policy is to exercise these restraints on the policy of the Atlantic powers. We must first accept the Cold War as the central fact of twentieth century politics (just as class war was the central fact of nineteenth-century politics) and then disprove the prophets who prove that it must end in World War III.

THE TRANSITION FROM CAPITALISM[1]
C. A. R. Crosland

I. The Theory of Capitalist Collapse

FIRST capitalism must be defined. For our purpose it is
sufficient to call it an advanced and industrialised society in
which the greater part of economic activity is undertaken by
privately-owned units, acting without interference by the state,
and under the incentive of private profit. It is, in other words,
an industrial system in which the ownership and control of real
capital are vested in a class of private 'capitalists', whose
economic decisions are taken in response to market influences
operating freely under conditions of *laisser-faire*.[2]

The left has traditionally believed, on the basis of the Marxist
analysis, that this system must, in time, collapse, and that
meanwhile the working class must suffer a worse and worse
impoverishment. But in fact capitalism has continued to expand
and the working class has enjoyed a constantly rising standard
of life. The British net national income, in real terms, had by
1938 increased to three and a half times its 1870 figure, and
income per head rose by two and a half times over the the same
perid. (Population growth accounts for the difference between
the two figures.) Real wages moved in line with income per
head, i.e. the proportionate share of wages in total income
remained constant, so that the working class was not even
growing relatively, still less absolutely, poorer.

Attempts have been made to salvage something from the
wreck by continuously moving forward the date at which decay
was due to set in. But no Marxist has dared to maintain that

---

[1] The analysis in this essay applies strictly only to Britain and to
similarly-placed mature industrialised countries.

[2] To define capitalism in this way as private ownership of real capital
plus a purely market economy does not mean that socialism can safely be
defined as the converse.

the 'inner contradictions' were not fully in operation during the inter-war decades—indeed, the poor performance of those two decades is always claimed in evidence. Yet even then the expansion continued, though at a lessened rate. The U.K. real national income rose by 31% during this period, and income per head by 21%. Again the working class shared fully in the rise, and real wages were over 20% higher in 1938 than in 1913. Even the great depression of 1931 did not arrest the trend—the U.K. national income was 20% higher in 1938 than in 1929, and output in the U.S. rose by 75% between 1929 and 1950.

These figures prove beyond doubt that the pre-war industrial system, for all its social injustices and unemployment, was economically still an expanding one. It is true that the American slump of 1931 went deeper than in previous cycles, and that recovery was less complete. But this, by itself, is not sufficient evidence of incipient decay. The 1931 depression, although unusually severe, was not the first depression of such severity—the famous slump of 1873–7 was at least as bad. And there are plenty of *ad hoc* explanations for the abnormally deflationary character of the whole inter-war period, e.g. the exceptional and depressing price relationship between primary and manufactured products, and in the U.S. in the nineteen-thirties the difficulties of adjustment to a completely transformed political situation.

None of this means that pre-war capitalism was in any way a satisfactory economic or social system, or that it was capable of continuing stability and full employment. It merely means that it could not be held to be in process of active decomposition, and thus likely to collapse of its own accord.

II. The Inevitable Transformation of Capitalism

But although it was foolish to expect the imminent demise of capitalism along the lines envisaged in Marxist theory, it was nevertheless possible to detect signs of a transformation in it. Up to 1939 these, though apparent and significant, were not of a fundamental character. But since 1945 the transformation

34

has gone much further, and it is now clear that capitalism is undergoing a metamorphosis into a quite different system, and that this is rendering academic most of the traditional socialist analysis.

The factors making for this transformation are quite natural and obvious ones, whose strength should occasion no surprise. By far the most important has been the increasingly effective reaction of the non-capitalist classes against the consequences of industrial *laisser-faire*—in particular, the recurrent unemployment, the insecurity, and the inequality. The growth, over the last fifty years, of powerful anti-capitalist movements—Labour and Socialist parties, non-Socialist radical parties, and organised trade unions—has had a cumulative effect. This has been most obvious where socialist governments have enjoyed long spells of power (Britain and the Scandinavian countries), but it has also been appreciable elsewhere. Strong socialist oppositions, periods of radical-reform governments (e.g. the New Deal in the U.S.), the continuous pressure of strong trade unions—these also have been sufficient, even without actual labour rule, to force modifications in the system; and indeed the capitalist parties themselves have more and more found it impossible to win elections without promising, and to a limited extent effecting, important changes. (None of this, of course, could have happened save in a democratic country; but then one of the errors the Marxists always made, on the basis of a faulty analysis of the nature of political conflict, was absurdly to underrate the socio-economic consequences of continued political democracy.)

But the pressure for change has not come solely from the anti-capitalist classes. It has been an illusion of the left to suppose that only the working class suffered from slumps and unemployment; of course, they suffer worst, but profits suffer too. It has been a further illusion that the capitalists would always choose passively to endure their losses rather than accept reform, and much too much was made in this connection of the opposition of the business class to the New Deal. In fact, the business class wants high profits, which are its whole

35

reason for existing; and to assume that it would continue indefinitely to dislike government action more than it disliked low profits was to assume an urge to suicide for which there is no warrant. The intellectuals of capitalism have long been prepared for drastic changes—Keynes wrote of the 'socialisation of investment', and Hansen has urged the 'socialisation of consumption'. These capitalist economists constitute the advance-guard, but the main body is also on the move. The change, as compared with the nineteen-thirties, in the attitude of the employing class to the needs of a full employment policy is already very striking, and there is no doubt that rather than endure a recurrence of deflation they will—in the end, reluctantly, and far too slowly—accept important limitations on the sovereignty of *laisser-faire*.

The resistance to change, moreover, has been weakened by the fact that the capitalist *bourgeoisie* is no longer as self-confident as in its heyday. It has, in Britain at least, lost its unquestioning faith in itself and in capitalism, and has been forced psychologically on to the defensive. This is largely due to the patent failures of capitalism as judged even by capitalist standards of success; no business-man who lived through the inter-war period could consider the system ideal from a purely self-interested point of view. It is also due to a bad conscience, induced by a crescendo of attacks and criticism, and indeed by the overwhelming evidence of social misery. The hunger marches, the soup-kitchens, the distressed areas of the nineteen-thirties have for ever destroyed the pristine certainty, so evident in the nineteenth century, that this was the best of all possible systems. The Churches (or some sections of them) have been influential in inculcating this sense of bad conscience, but perhaps even more effective has been the Trojan horse of the Turnstile Intelligentsia; the fact that it was so fashionable to be politically left before the war is a sure sign that the educated class had lost its former faith.

Few now would accept, what was universally believed a century ago and what is, after all, the basic theoretical tenet of capitalist dogma, that the unfettered pursuit of monetary gain must, by the operation of the 'invisible hand', lead to the 'optimum' amount and distribution of economic welfare; and the belief in the absolute rights of property, always one of the essential characteristics of capitalist ideology, has been infinitely weakened over recent decades. Savage taxation of income and property, and the nationalisation of private industries, have aroused scarcely more opposition than measures to limit child labour a hundred years ago; and, very significantly, the opposition has been couched in terms not so much of interference with property rights as of the effects on economic efficiency. This shift in the argument from the ideological to the technical plane shows how far the self-confidence of capitalism has been undermined.

In addition, the nature of capitalist development has itself brought certain basic changes. The growth of size in business, combined with laws of limited liability, has meant a wide dispersion of shareholding. The classical *entrepreneur*, the familiar owner-manager, is gradually disappearing; under the joint-stock form of organisation property-owning, once an active role, has sunk to merely passive shareholding, while decision-making and economic control have passed to the new class of (largely) non-owning managers. The propertied class has thus lost its traditional capitalist function—the exploitation with its own capital of the techniques of production—and as the function disappears, so the power slips away.

On top of all these developments came two world wars, which greatly hastened the pace of change. The necessity for planning and the discovery that it gave successful results, the detailed control of industry by government, the impetus to left-wing movements and reforms—these made it quite impossible for the system to revert, on either occasion, to the relative purity of pre-war days.

Thus capitalism, with no hope of abortion, is forced to give birth to a new society: first, because the political pressures against it are so strong as to make its position untenable; secondly, because the capitalist class has lost the will to resist of its confident heyday; thirdly, because in any case the absolute

37

power of private property has had to give way, under the impact of technical change, to managerial control.

These influences—part external, part self-generated—have proved, in combination, irresistible. The speed of change has varied through time (being greater in depression and less in prosperity, and greatest of all in periods of Labour rule), but the trend has been consistent and unmistakable. It is now quite clear that capitalism has not the strength to resist the process of metamorphosis into a qualitatively different kind of society.

III. *The Post-capitalist Society*

I propose to list eight essential features of this new society, choosing those which distinguish it from capitalism.

(1) Individual property rights no longer constitute the essential basis of economic and social power. Under capitalism, it was the owners of the means of production who were the obvious ruling class. To-day, with active ownership converted into passive shareholding, control has passed elsewhere, and much of the traditional socialist-capitalist dispute is now irrelevant. The ownership of property is still germane, naturally, to all questions of the distribution of wealth, but (as the Nazi revolution had already shown) it is no longer true that property relationships determine the distribution of economic power.

(2) The power previously wielded by the owners of property has now largely, though not entirely, passed to the class of managers—working directors, managing directors, and the higher grades of salaried executives. The significant fact about this class is that it neither (*a*) itself draws its main income from property, nor (*b*) predominantly owns the businesses which it controls; and it is this, combined with the abdication of control by the now passive owners, which justifies one in speaking of a transfer of power from ownership to management.

This transfer of power does not, *by itself*, constitute the major revolution that some writers (Burnham, Drucker, *et al.*) have supposed. The new managers largely have the same social origins and social attitudes as the *entrepreneurs* whom they replace.

But the curtailment in the rights of property is significant in two respects. Especially in the larger firms, there is less tenderness towards the demands of shareholders, and higher dividends are certainly not the main incentive to expansion. (This is very relevant to Government economic policy.) As a corollary, the attitude to the State is much less hostile. Co-operation comes more easily to the new managers than the old; they are, no doubt, suspicious still, but there is little of the violent hostility which would have been apparent in the vigorous days of free capitalism. Indeed, it has been a subject for comment that the removal of Government controls is often greeted with much less than unanimous enthusiasm by the industry concerned.

(3) The power of the State has enormously increased, and it is now an independent intermediate power, dominating the economic life of the country. The forms that state intervention takes are primarily three: direct state operation of certain limited sectors of industry, physical controls over the remaining private sectors, and the use of budgetary policy to determine the total level of income, the distribution of that income, and (occasionally) the distribution of resources between different uses. Another essential feature of capitalism has thus disappeared—the absolute autonomy of economic life. This one change alone would justify the statement that the capitalist era has now passed into history.

(4) The level of social services is now so high that our present society is often called the Welfare State. This has far-reaching consequences. It removes the insecurity which made so strongly for social discontent; it involves (since it is financed partly by high taxation of the rich) more equality than would be the case in a low-tax *laisser-faire* economy: and it makes inevitable (owing to the level of taxation involved) a high degree of governmental intervention in economic affairs

(5) The trend of employment is towards a high level, and a recurrence of chronic mass unemployment is most unlikely. The Keynesian techniques are now well understood, and there is no reason to fear a repetition of the New Deal experience of a government with the will to spend its way out of depression, but

39

frustrated in so doing by faulty knowledge. The political pressure for full employment is stronger than ever before; the experience of the inter-war years bit so deeply into the political psychology of the nation that full employment, if threatened, would always constitute the dominant issue at any election, and no right-wing party could now survive a year in office if it permitted the figures of unemployment which were previously quite normal.

Certain characteristic features of the post-capitalist society will also help to sustain employment as compared with the position under capitalism. Generous social services and a more equal division of income will diminish the volume of savings and provide a permanent cushion of demand. The increased economic activity of the state means that over a large part of industry investment will remain steady instead of fluctuating cyclically in response to changing profit-expectations, and this in turn will exert a steadying effect on the private sector.

The strength of reforming tendencies will ensure a high level of social investment in housing, education, new towns, etc. And the needs of colonial development, combined with permanently worsened terms of trade, will make for buoyant exports in place of the chronic export-trade depression which was always dragging the economy down before the war.

It is not likely, therefore, that we shall experience in the new economy anything like the 14% average of unemployment which characterised inter-war Britain. That is not to say, of course, that every Conservative government will keep employment at the level of the last few years; such a government would have far more scruple about using the available techniques, and no doubt would be slow to do so. But it does mean that the underlying trend will be healthier than under free capitalism, and that such fluctuations as persist will take place round a much higher average level.

This is not, after all, a very surprising conclusion. Most economists would agree that an uncontrolled but highly capitalised society not only had no natural automatic tendency to rest at a full employment level, but actually had a positive bias towards instability. It was the combination of complete *laisser-faire* with consequent instability, and a very high savings ratio due to the unequal division of wealth, which led to low and fluctuating employment levels under capitalism. But in the post-capitalist society both these factors are drastically modified. The Welfare State calls for higher and more redistributive taxation, and thus increases spending at the expense of saving; while the enlarged economic activity of the state ensures a high and steady level of public or state-induced demand. *Laisser-faire* gives way to what Hansen has called the dual-production and dual-consumption economy, i.e. an economy in which both production and consumption decisions are shared between a public and a private sector. Such an economy is far more likely to give rise to chronic inflation than chronic deflation.

(6) The trend of production, and therefore of the standard of living, is strongly upward. Previous sections have made it clear that even the depressions of free capitalism were not sufficient to arrest the continued rise in real income. There is still less reason to expect it to be arrested in the post-capitalist world: indeed, the opposite is much more likely. Economic depression of the inter-war kind, even though impotent to counteract entirely the forces making for expansion, quite certainly damps down the rate of expansion. Because profit-expectations are low, the level of capital expenditure is also low, and productivity rises less than it otherwise would. Both sides of industry, in a search for security and a reaction against the cut-throat competition which depression initially breeds, take eagerly to restrictive practices, and cartel arrangements flourish.

But under a high level of employment, investment is held high, and restrictive practices decline as they become less necessary; moreover, as labour is both scarce and dear, more economical methods of production are encouraged. Certainly the once popular view that full employment, though obviously desirable on short-term welfare grounds, might exact a high price in the long run through its effects on incentives, finds no support from the productivity figures in post-war Britain,

It is falling markets which encourage restrictionism and go-slow, while high demand and buoyant markets induce an atmosphere more favourable to innovation and expansion. Under the higher employment provided by the mixed economy it will be surprising if the national income does not rise annually by more than the $1\frac{1}{2}\%$ which was the norm before the war.

(7) The class structure of society is more than ever variegated, and the classical outlines characteristic of early capitalism give way to a baroque profusion of detail. The (to Marx very unexpected) rise of the technical and professional middle class is largely responsible. This is likely to continue. Increased mechanisation constantly reduces the size of the strict factory working class; a higher standard of life creates a continuously-increasing demand for services as opposed to goods; and in any case middle-class psychology and standards are steadily spreading far outside the bounds of that class itself. Thus a vast amorphous cushion of intermediate classes is interposed between the top and bottom strata, and softens the struggle between them.

(8) Ideologically, the dominant emphasis ceases to be on the rights of property, private initiative, competition, and the profit-motive; and is transferred to the duties of the state, social and economic security, and the virtues of co-operative action.

It can readily be seen from this list of features that the new society is quite different in kind from the capitalism which it succeeds—and also that it is very similar to post-war British or Scandinavian society after several years of Labour government. Even in pre-war Britain the transformation had begun, and right-wing governments could only delay and not resist it altogether. Under the post-war Labour administration the tempo of change was enormously accelerated, and by 1951 Britain had, in all the essentials, ceased to be a capitalist country. In Sweden also the change was virtually complete.

What should the new society be called? All manner of names

suggest themselves or are suggested: the Welfare State, the Mixed Economy, the Managerial State, Progressive Capitalism, Fair Dealism, State Capitalism, the First Stage of Socialism, the New Society being born in the Womb of the Old, and so on to the limits of one's verbal imagination. Differences of opinion about the right nomenclature will partly reflect merely ideological differences; because different people want to see in the new society a likeness to the system they themselves support (whether socialism or capitalism), they choose a name which is from this point of view persuasive.

But there is a genuine difficulty about classifying this form of society because it is so essentially a mixed one so far as the traditional categories are concerned. It is capitalist to the extent that private ownership of industry predominates, that most production is for the market, and that many of the old class divisions persist. It is non-capitalist to the extent that market influences are subordinated to central planning, not over the whole detailed field of labour and production, but in certain strategically decisive sectors; that the power of the state is much greater than that of any one particular class; and that the distribution of the national income is consciously a matter of political decision and not the automatic consequence of market forces. It is managerial to the extent that the control of industry has largely passed (subject to state controls) into the hands of the managerial class, which has usurped the position of the old capitalist class. It is socialist in that the distribution of income is far more egalitarian, that much economic power and parts of industry are socialised, that a national minimum and a welfare cushion exist, and that planning is largely directed to traditional socialist ends. It is, in fact, economically and socially, a pluralist society.

For all these difficulties, some name must be found, and the best that I can suggest is Statism. The name is ugly, and has too unfavourable a ring. But the most fundamental change from capitalism is the change from *laisser-faire* to state control, and it is as well to have a name which spotlights this crucial change.

Statism, then, is the form of society which, in Britain at least,

43

is in process of succeeding to capitalism. It represents, without doubt, an impressive advance as judged by Socialist standards. Its more effective control over the level of employment, and the consequent gain in stability and output, make it if not immune from, at least much less vulnerable to, the strains and stresses inherent in any industrial society. The higher employment, generous social services, less flagrant inequalities of wealth and opportunity—in all these ways the new society is infinitely more humane and decent than the old. Most of the unbearable social tensions which afflicted capitalism will have disappeared; there will be no repetition of Jarrow and Ebbw Vale, dole queues and hunger-marches, to inspire violent feelings and actions in the working class, whose relative gains are, indeed, significantly large. Both the area, and the bitterness, of social conflict are much reduced.

An additional reason for expecting greater social peace is that power in the new society will be very widely diffused. Economic power, in the Marxist sense of control over the means of production, is distributed amongst the old capitalists (in smaller-scale industry), the new managers, the State machine, the shareholders, the executives of the public boards, and (very important) the organised workers (especially with the inevitable trend towards more workers' control in industry). With this dispersion of control, no one class can lever itself, as the capitalist class for so long did, into a dominantly possessive relationship to the means of production.

The corollary of this in the social field is that in contrast to the classical Marxist picture of two tightly-knit homogeneous social classes ranged clearly against each other, we find a very complicated class structure with an increasing proliferation of middle groups. And since political power also will be evenly balanced, and alternate between left and right, there will, in my view, be no uniquely delineated ruling class, nor clearly defined class struggle. Given this equilibrium in the balance of forces, the less violent pressure for change, and the reversion, after a brief abnormal spell of *laisser-faire*, to the normal historical pattern (both in the ancient and the modern world) of

44

conscious control over social and economic life, the new society may prove to be a very enduring one.

IV. *Other theories of the Succession*

The notion that capitalism is passing peacefully into statism will require a considerable mental adjustment from those many socialists whose ideas are still coloured by Marxist determinism. No single aspect of Marxism had made so deep an impression on the consciousness of the left as the belief that socialism must, after however long or stormy a transition, inevitably succeed to capitalism.

But there was never really any cogent reason for accepting this cheering belief in the historical necessity of socialism. It had to rest on two premises: first, that capitalism must inevitably disappear, and, secondly, that no possible successor other than socialism existed.

The first of these premises, as we have seen, is not absurd (although the Marxist version of it is). But the second was always insecurely based. Often it depended merely on reading carefully-chosen values into the meaningless syllogism of thesis, antithesis, and therefore synthesis. Sometimes it rested (as Duehring pointed out) on the purely mystical notion of the negation of the negation. Or else it required a tautological definition of socialism—first define capitalism as a system of absolute private property rights (which is reasonable), then prove the inevitability of the destruction of these absolute rights (which is also not unplausible), and then define socialism as any society in which these rights are absent. But any other than a tautological definition of socialism as the system which succeeds capitalism must allow the possibility of the disappearance of the one without the advent of the other.

At its strongest, the theory rested on the particular Marxist version of the last days of capitalism. Once given a breakdown in the system that put it quite beyond repair, and given, too, a polarisation of classes so complete that an enormous and impoverished proletariat alone faced the disintegrating

45

bourgeoisie, then socialism clearly would emerge from the resulting explosion (though even this requires a dubious definition of socialism as the assumption of power by the proletariat). But there is not the slightest chance, as we have seen, of either of these conditions being fulfilled.

There is obviously, then, no reason in logic or history why the succession should inevitably pass to socialism, and in any event, as a matter of hard fact, it is currently passing to statism.

It is of no use to evade the argument by maintaining that statism is not a new society at all, but only a minor modification of capitalism. On the contrary, statism represents a major social revolution. With its arrival, the most characteristic features of capitalism have all disappeared: the absolute rule of private property, the subjection of the whole of economic life to market influences, the domination of the profit motive, the neutrality of government, the typical *laisser-faire* division of income, and the ideology of individual rights. This is no minor modification: it is a major historical change.

It is quite true that the change is not as *revolutionary-looking*, on the surface, as the sharp transition to full-blooded capitalism in the first half of the nineteenth century. The normal pattern of men's lives is less disturbed, and there is not the same upheaval and uprooting. But this is not because the change is less revolutionary in terms of class and power relationships. It is merely because the statist revolution, unlike the final stages of the capitalist revolution, is not accompanied by a sensational change in economic technique. It was the advent of factory industrialism, rather than the advent of capitalism *per se*, which gave the sense of cataclysmic upheaval. This time there is no disruptive alteration in techniques, and so the process seems much quieter. And so, after all, would the transition (unless collapse and violent revolt are predicated) to socialism. All three are industrial societies, and this common element provides a sense and appearance of continuity.

Even if there were no statism to provide empirical proof that capitalism and socialism are not successive stations on a one-way line, it would be provided by fascism and communism.

46

Fascism in Germany was a society qualitatively different from either capitalism or socialism, and it succeeded by revolution to a highly-developed capitalism. Communism in Russia is certainly not socialism by any definition current in the West, yet it now holds power; though here the proof is less convincing, since pre-1914 Russia was not a characteristically capitalist society. But statism, fascism and communism between them leave little intact of the exclusive capitalism-socialism dichotomy.

The alternative successor to capitalism which both recent history and current writing suggest as a possibility is the dictatorial managerial society, or (to use Laurat's ponderous but useful terminology) totalitarian bureau-technocracy or pluto-technocracy.

The managerial state, as it has appeared in practice and in the writings of its prophets, has the following characteristics: (i) state ownership of industrial property, or else state control so complete that the locus of ownership is irrelevant (as under the Nazi property laws); (ii) complete centralisation of economic decision, the market economy being replaced by a detailed budget of production; (iii) a clearly-defined and all-powerful new ruling class of managers (state bureaucrats and industrial executives) having absolute control over the means of production, and using their control, like any other untrammelled ruling class, to give themselves preferential treatment and perpetuate their rule; and (iv) total absence of political democracy and the traditional liberties. This managerial society is quite different in kind from capitalism, statism or socialism. It has already made its appearance in Nazi Germany and Stalinist Russia, and its certain and universal triumph has been the subject of many Burnhamite prophecies.

We are not concerned with whether the managerial state is a desirable successor—obviously, no socialist would choose it in preference to statism (let alone socialism)—but whether it is a likely one. To answer this question, two forms of it need to be distinguished.

First, communism, i.e. the particular brand of totalitarian

47

'bureau-technocracy' which Communist Parties establish when they come into power. This is a product of a revolutionary situation (created characteristically by war) in a country politically and economically backward (and therefore with no democratic system and tradition): and of the seizure of power by a revolutionary group (with or without mass support) which is ideologically Leninist (i.e. any Communist Party anywhere) and is successful because all other groups are inchoate and disorganised. Thus, to be accurate, one should say, turning the classical Marxist postulate on its head, that communism can by definition only replace a pre-capitalist society, since this combination of conditions can never be present under an advanced capitalism. A 'spontaneous' communist succession, therefore, (i.e. ignoring its possible arrival in the wake of the Red Army) can be ruled out so far as the industrial countries are concerned. Communism belongs properly to the problem of under-developed societies, as one of the possible media through which they develop a modern and rational economic system.

The other possible version of managerial revolution is along the lines made familiar by James Burnham. This version differs from communism in two essential respects (although the ultimate end-product is similar). First, the leaders of the revolution are *ab initio* a managerial class, an upper group in society, and they at no stage represent, as communism initially purports to do, a movement from below: it is rather a palace revolution of one section of the ruling class against another. Secondly, the Burnhamite revolution can by definition only take place in a mature capitalist country, since only there does a sufficient managerial class exist—under communism the revolution only gradually *grows into* a managerial society.

There is no need to parade Burnham's argument in detail. It is tempting to rebut it merely by pointing to the many individual prophecies which have already been falsified by events. But analytically the argument has serious flaws. First, like Marx, Burnham accepts the inevitability of capitalist breakdown as a result of worsening unemployment. But if this view is rejected, much of his analysis falls automatically to the ground.

Secondly, he assumes that the managerial class is much more close-knit and clearly-delineated than in fact it is. The tangle of social relationships is much more complicated than he supposes, and it is very *simpliste* (and much too Marxist) to isolate the managers so sharply from other social groups.

Thirdly, the 'managers' are much too divided in their political loyalties to wish to carry out a managerial revolution. It is not true that they are bitterly and necessarily hostile to capitalism. They may mildly dislike the *rentiers*, and be irritated by the claims of shareholders; but they are far too prosperous ever to become a revolutionary force. It would not, to them, be worth a great upheaval merely to destroy the nominal shareholding rights of the *ci-devant* capitalist class—any more than the victorious capitalist class, having won its battle in 1832, bothered to eliminate the landowning aristocracy. After all, there are plenty of capitalist Lord John Russells to lead a managerial party.

Burnham provided a brilliant (though often exaggerated) analysis of the transfer of power within industry from the owning to the managing class. But this alone does not add up to the managerial state as he conceived it, and I do not believe in the advent of this state unless (which I have already argued is unlikely) capitalism fails to transform itself, or be transformed, and lurches instead into increasingly violent crises of the sort which Marx expected, but which Burnham's managers might more probably exploit. (The same circumstances might arise for reasons outside the socio-economic field, e.g. a moral and physical collapse due to defeat in war.)

Thus statism still appears as much the most likely successor.

V. *External Factors*

So far, current developments in the British and similar economies have been treated in isolation. I have abstracted from international factors, and the analysis has been in terms of a 'closed system'. This is justifiable and necessary in order to isolate the dominant internal trends, but the time has now come to consider whether there are any external influences at work which are likely to arrest or divert those internal trends.

First, and most obvious, is the Cold War. What effect would a generation of high rearmament have on the prospects outlined above? The answer is, much less than most people expect. The whole question is, for the moment, hopelessly out of perspective as a result of recent disputes about our short-term capacity to rearm. But considered in long-run terms no economic problem exists. Rearmament consists initially in levering the economy from a position in which $x\%$ of the national product is spent on arms to a position where $x+y\%$ is so spent. During this process, which in the present case will take from three to four years, the whole of the annual rise in output—and possibly something more—is required for arms. At the end of the period the desired position of $x+y\%$ is reached, and thereafter the economy remains geared to this level of expenditure. But since it is an absolute level of arms production, and not a proportion, which is really being aimed at, the annual rise in output is from that moment again available for civilian use, and the upward movement in real income begins once more. The effect of rearmament on the standard of life is merely to abstract three years' (or four or five, if one wishes to be gloomy) increase in output. Catastrophic as this may be in its immediate political effects, the long-run consequences, viewed over a generation of time, are not significant.[1]

In certain ways the effects of rearmament will, paradoxically enough, be on balance beneficial. The danger of unemployment is still further reduced, and the extent of government planning increased. The Cold War will necessarily, just as did the last two shooting wars, give a strong impetus to statist tendencies, and not even a right-wing government, under its impact, would be able to hold back a rapid movement away from *laisser-faire*. Peace, alas, is a less good lubricant than war of the engine of social change.

[1] I assume, what is certainly the case, that the present three-year increase in the arms-ratio cannot be repeated several times without the Cold War developing into actual war—and that is a possibility which lies outside my province of discussion.

Secondly, a severe worsening of the terms of trade might wholly or partially offset the internal factors making for higher income. Rising population and incomes in the primary-producing countries, it is sometimes argued, combined with the phenomenal demand for raw materials which expanding industrial output must involve, will lead to the prices of primary products rising sharply relative to those of manufactured goods, with a consequent fall in the standard of life in the industrial countries.

These trends are certainly at work. But some of the alarmism current about future raw material supplies may be exaggerated. This is not the first time since the industrial revolution that dark fears have been expressed on this score, without the expected catastrophe in fact materialising. New sources of supply are discovered, and high prices induce a higher output. In industry the effects of scarcity are mitigated or overcome by substitution and more efficient use (cf. the rise in rayon production in 1951 despite the much-feared shortfall in sulphur supplies). One should not underrate the copious fertility of the modern chemist in perfecting synthetic substitutes, nor the continued ingenuity of industrial science; synthetic rubber, chemicals from oil, atomic energy—such discoveries prove the unwisdom of taking a static view of raw material requirements. The main problem lies not in the field of fuel and metal materials, but of food and agricultural materials. This is a problem which *can* be solved, given a sufficient readiness on the part of the advanced nations to invest in the under-developed areas. Whether it *will* be solved is a matter of speculation. It might be that disaster is just round the corner; it might be that present scarcities will be completely overcome, as has happened in the past. The most likely outcome is perhaps half-way between these two extremes. Cheap food and materials will not return, and Britain will not again enjoy the highly advantageous terms of trade of the nineteen-thirties. On the other hand, the effect on future living standards may not be disastrous. We have already sustained a very sharp deterioration as compared with pre-war, and absorbed its effects on

51

real income. There may be a further worsening still in store, but it is hard to believe that it will do more than abstract a few years' increase in productivity from home consumption. It may retard, but will not prevent, the rise in Western standards of life.

We should certainly not, as socialists, cavil at the contrast with the nineteen-thirties. Better terms of trade for primary producers represent a continuing and automatic World Plan for Mutual Aid and movement toward world equalisation of income. And it has to be remembered that unfavourable terms of trade for manufacturing producers, tiresome as they may be from a short-term real income point of view, have the compensation that they create highly favourable conditions for exports and so for total employment. The unusual severity of the inter-war depression was not unconnected with terms of trade so unfavourable to the primary producers that they were far too poor to buy the volume of imports needed to give full employment in the industrial countries.

Thirdly, the U.S.A.—the great external question-mark. But the U.S. needs a section to itself.

VI. *The Role of America*

U.S. affairs are seldom discussed on the British left with any degree of objectivity. Too many emotional prejudices are involved, and judgments are biassed by immense sub-conscious efforts at projection and displacement.

Nevertheless, answers are required to two distinct but inter-related questions. First, is the U.S. also moving towards statism? Secondly, will developments in the U.S. be such as to distort the spontaneous internal trends in Britain and similarly placed countries?

Until 1929 the U.S. remained the classic prototype of pure capitalism—an extraordinary instance of the combined strength and weakness of that now-dying social form. But, under the impact of the worst slump in living memory, came the New Deal—the product of irresistible electoral pressure, which met for some time with half-frightened acquiescence from a puzzled business class which had entirely lost its bearings. At the end of the decade, when otherwise reaction might have set in, there came the war, and after the war the Truman Fair Deal, and the gains were in consequence consolidated.

From the political storms and stresses which accompanied the Roosevelt era one might suppose that a major social revolution had occurred. But, in retrospect, what does the New Deal amount to? In origin it was not a planned consistent left-wing programme of reform, but a confused attempt to deal *ad hoc* with a major depression. Its permanent legacy was a significant shift in the balance of power consequent on the enormous growth of trade union strength: a relatively advanced system of social security: a certain increase in the influence of the state, and in particular a permanently larger Budget than before.

These changes were all important and all in a radical direction; and judged in the light of American history they seemed at the time to be revolutionary. But once set beside the account of the statist society (see p. 38), their limited character becomes apparent. They represent only a modification of capitalism, only a first step along the road that leads to statism.

What of the future? There is, certainly, an observable trend towards statism, but it is weaker than its counterpart in Europe. The most apparent difference from Europe is that the political pressure for change is much less strong. There exists, it is true, a sizeable and growing literature in advocacy of the 'mixed economy', which in effect is the American term for statism. But there exists no socialist party pressing for major change. The Democratic Party is only radical spasmodically and in parts, and in any event finds it difficult to obtain a majority for further advance as opposed to the defence of past achievements. And even the trade unions appear to want a reformed and refurbished capitalism, rather than its supersession by another system.

The reasons for this are not obscure. Partly they lie in a number of familiar social factors—the failure of American capitalism to develop a rigid class system on the British model,

53

the relatively egalitarian system of education, a high degree of equal opportunity in industry, the persistence of the 'frontier' mentality, etc. But the dominant reason—indeed, the outstanding feature of the whole American scene—is the extraordinary productive achievement of U.S. capitalism. Aided by many natural advantages, the American economy has turned out, despite and across the most violent fluctuations, an enormous and rapidly increasing supply of goods and services. Areas of poverty still exist, but a survey of the whole scene shows a level of real wages which is incomparably the highest in the world, and still increasing at a noticeable rate. While this continues to be the case, and while the door to industrial promotion remains wide open, it is hard to conceive of the unions turning to bite the hand that feeds them so lavishly—and capitalism can survive any pressures against itself that do not draw strength from the organised workers' movement.

Not only are the pressures against it weaker than in Europe, but its defences are incomparably stronger. Now that the reforms of the last twenty years have cured the worst abuses of the system, Americans have recovered the self-confidence which temporarily forsook them during the great depression. And to-day one of the results of the communist offensive has been to evoke a still more ardent faith in liberal capitalism. At home belief in the American way of life becomes more fanatical with every communist attack; abroad, countless E.C.A. officials, business-men, and visiting trade unionists preach the doctrine of mass production for mass markets and a rising standard of life—essentially, in American eyes, a capitalist ideology. And there is no doubt whatever of the strong conviction that lies behind these (perfectly legitimate) attempts to proselytise. Trade unionists are at one with business-men in believing that mass-production private capitalism offers the world's best answer to poverty and unrest—and believing, too, that it is a progressive and revolutionary system compared with many of the backward class-ridden regimes they find in Europe and elsewhere.

The weaker pressures and the stronger defences, as compared with Europe, both derive essentially from the same fact, that

American capitalism has so far been capable of offering so high a standard of life that the case for it, even to the bulk of the working population, seems stronger than the case for change. It is as much as the liberal movement can do to hold the modifications and improvements of the present Fair Deal position. The further transition to statism will either take a century, or not occur at all—*unless* (and these are two crucial conditions) either the Cold War and high rearmament persist for twenty years, in which case statism will make a gradual entry, or the U.S. reverts to pre-war figures of unemployment. This second possibility raises the other question posed above—namely, whether developments in the U.S. will be such as to disrupt stability in the world outside.

One can be sure, at the outset, that the American economy, as at present organised, is not capable of sustaining a stable level of full employment. With *laisser-faire* still hardly limited, and the power of the state so weak, it is certain that the U.S. is still too typically a capitalist country to avoid continued cyclical fluctuations. But of how violent a character?

It is my belief that these fluctuations will not be of the same severity as was the case between the wars, and that they will take place round a higher average level of employment. The following are some of the reasons for this belief.

(1) Social security payments provide a cushion of demand which has not existed in the past.

(2) The farm support programme, which neither party could conceivably jettison, sets a very high floor to any possible fall in farmers' incomes. The importance of this can be gauged by the fact that agricultural depression was possibly the biggest single deflationary factor in the American economy between the wars.

(3) The new role of the U.S. in world affairs will ensure a higher volume both of arms expenditure and of foreign aid directly related to the requirements of diplomacy.

(4) The new ideology of inter-governmental charity and the development of backward areas will require continued governmental outlays.

All these affect the size of the Budget. They have not yet attained their full potential scale, but their significance can be assessed from the fact that already in 1949 (before the recent rearmament programme) the Federal Budget reached a figure of over $40 billion, compared with $9 billion at the height of the New Deal spending. It is not easy to imagine a 1932 catastrophe with a Budget of this magnitude.

(5) A strong cheap money psychology now exists, and the long-term rate of interest is low.

(6) A minor revolution in the distribution of income has occurred over the last two decades. This has been much too little remarked upon in Britain. In 1929 the top 5% of income-recipients took 34% of the total post-tax income of individuals; by 1939 they were taking only 27% and by 1946 their share had dropped to 18%. This remarkable growth of income equality will mean a less unmanageable volume of savings, and a higher and steadier level of consumption demand.

(7) As compared with the early 'thirties, public opinion has greatly hardened on the subject of full employment. It no longer passively accepts the view that nothing can be done, and were a slump to begin the political (and trade union) pressure on the Government to act would be irresistible. Even Congressional opinion has moved; a Full Employment Act is on the Statute Book and, for all its lack of teeth, this is a sign that times have changed.

(8) The techniques of anti-depression policy are now well understood, and action when it came would be more effective than the gallant but chaotic efforts of the Roosevelt Government. A vast literature on compensatory fiscal policy now exists, and this has had its influence on governmental thinking. It is always unwise, in any event, to underrate the American capacity for rapid changes in policy to meet an unexpected situation. The revolution of thought required, and the amount of difficult improvisation, would be far less than was involved in the complete *bouleversement* in the American attitude to world affairs between 1946 and 1948.

This is a very different picture from the nineteen-thirties: of

an economy still liable to swings, but held now within certain
limits by defences on either side. Nobody expects the U.S.
permanently to hold its present record level of employment,
and the slump at the close of rearmament may well be serious.
But the magnitude of the depressions to be expected, though
large enough to cause periodic disturbances and recurrent
dollar problems in the rest of the world, should not be such
as to set off ungovernable downward movements of the 1931
variety, or to prevent a secular upward trend of income in
Great Britain.

To revert, in conclusion, to the question of U.S. internal
trends. Nobody but a very unwise person (or an economist)
would attempt to put figures on the likely range of these future
fluctuations. But without a somewhat exact view of this range
it is hopeless to speculate on the future of American capitalism.
If the down-turns are all as mild as the 1949 recession, they will
make too little impact on the public mind, and nothing will
change. If, as is more likely, they are a good deal more serious
than this, though without reaching the catastrophic depths of
1932, then we may expect the pressures against capitalism, and
making for statism, to be at least periodically strong. In that
event, the same developments may gradually occur in the U.S.
as have already occurred in Britain—though at an infinitely
slower pace, and probably without throwing up the same
political forms (e.g. without the emergence of a politically
separate Labour Party). But this must remain a most tentative
conclusion. No kind of prophecy about America has a longer
history of unredeemed wrongness than that based on analogy
with Britain.

VII. From Statism to Socialism

In the course of achieving statism, British Labour has put
into effect a very large part of its traditional programme, and
a typical Labour speech of the nineteen-thirties to-day reads
like a catalogue of post-war legislation. But the consequence of
success, as so often, is bewilderment—as to where we go from

here, whether we wish to advance much further, and what (if anything) there is of socialism which statism does not already give. These questions must be answered if Labour is to recover its lost sense of direction. But first two matters must be cleared out of the way which otherwise might obfuscate the major issue. First, it has to be understood that the 1951 dissension between Gaitskellites and Bevanites has no relevance for the future of socialism. The right level of arms expenditure, raw material supplies, teeth and spectacles, marginal increases in subsidies—all these were important questions in the context of the time, but all were a product of a particular situation created by rearmament. They raised no issue of long-term principle, nor threw into relief the direction of future advance.

Secondly, interludes of Tory rule will always tend to still doubts and silence questions about the ultimate content of socialism. Each Tory government will react some way—not to the extent of dismantling the whole structure of statism, but certainly to the extent of making breaches in it. The defence of past achievements will then provide a sufficient rallying cry, and the repair and consolidation of statism an ample programme of immediate action.

The question of Tory reaction perhaps calls for a comment. The right will turn back the clock on each occasion for a variety of reasons. Partly these will be ideological—attachment to capitalist values is still strong in some sections of the Conservative party, though not in others. Partly it is a cultural time-lag; even though the whole business community must find far healthier trading conditions in the high employment which statism brings, yet some sections are slow to realise the fact, or else are still suspicious that the full employment policy (which may include deficit finance and similar unorthodox measures) will lead not to prosperity but to disaster.

Partly it is a quite logical dislike of the shift in the locus of economic power from the board-rooms of industry to the state machine in Whitehall, and a feeling that dangerous precedents are being established, and forces set in motion which may later threaten the whole principle of private industry. And lastly—

strongest feeling of all—there is an intense distaste for the type of fiscal policy which the Welfare State demands. Social services and redistribution mean near-penal rates of income and profits taxation, and the hostility of the wealthier classes and of industry to a level of taxation which so threatens their standards and conventions is quite enough to breed a strong desire for 'return to normalcy'.

For these reasons, each Tory government will certainly beat a retreat (in particular toward greater inequality) from the position reached under the previous Labour administration. But the retreat will be half-hearted. The pressures making for statism are far too strong to be held back, and the Tories too intuitive a party indefinitely to play Canute. The right-wing sabotage of Labour's programme, which every Left Book Club member expected before the war, never in fact materialised. For precisely the same reason, the Conservatives now cannot and will not restore completely the pre-war *status quo*.

However, these partial retreats will provide plenty of material for Labour speeches and election programmes. So also, indeed, quite apart from Tory retreats, will reforms demanding to be accomplished within the broad framework of statism. Much could be done on the periphery of affairs, and without affecting the essential character of our society, to make the system more efficient. Action against monopoly, reforms in the marketing structure, the extension of development councils, improvements in the nationalised industries, more efficient planning techniques for running a full employment economy—these are only some of the spheres in which fresh action is desirable and possible. Here again is plenty to fill an election programme.

But none of these issues is fundamental to the long-term question, or gives any guidance as to how far and in what direction socialists should wish to advance beyond the present achievement.

The answer clearly depends on how socialism is defined. One now popular type of definition provides an immediate answer. A representative example—though there are many others—is the Frankfurt declaration of the reborn Socialist

International in 1951, in which (after a preamble, so vague as to be almost meaningless, about an end to 'the exploitation of man by man') the whole emphasis is placed on democratic planning, which is regarded as the basic condition of socialism. Now what is significant about this declaration is that socialism, as here defined, already largely obtains under statism. The worker can no longer be said to be exploited, and the declared objects of planning (defined in the manifesto as 'full employment, higher production, a rising standard of life, social security and a fair distribution of income and property') are (at least if one omits the one word 'property') in process of achievement. The name may still be Socialism, but the features look uncommonly like those of the Welfare State.

This type of definition represents a natural enough tendency. The planned full-employment Welfare State is the outcome of the first successful spells of majority Labour government anywhere, and it is tempting to assume that its achievement must constitute the final goal for socialists everywhere. It is, all are agreed, a great advance on pre-war capitalism, and to socialist parties which have never been in power it seems to promise gains of overwhelming significance when measured against conditions in their own countries. And at least such definitions represent a welcome advance in realism when compared with the chosen phrases from Marx or Kautsky which have so far served to define the goals of socialist action.

But to accept this approach involves maintaining that socialism was to all intents and purposes achieved (apart from certain temporary difficulties connected with rearmament) in the Britain of 1951—or at least that it would have been achieved after a few more years of progress along the same lines. There are those on the right of the Party (and in Scandinavia also) who would maintain precisely this, especially amongst the many liberal-minded people who joined the Party in horror at the unemployment and industrial poverty of the nineteen-thirties. The Labour Party would then become essentially a party for the defence of the 1951 position, with perhaps a few more minor reforms thrown in to sweeten the temper of the rank and file.

Nobody can argue that such an attitude is *wrong*, since it is based on a normative judgment, and is therefore not open to logical disproof. But it is safe to say that it does not represent the view of the majority of socialists, and, since it does not concur with my own view either, I shall assume that socialism still means a society different in kind, not only from capitalism, but also from the statism of 1951.

I shall rule two definitions out as commanding no support—the Marxist 'nationalisation of the means of production, distribution and exchange', and the early Fabian emphasis on collectivism—and shall choose, as probably the highest common factor of agreement, a definition by Professor Cole in 1935:

By Socialism I mean a form of society in which men and women are not divided into opposing economic classes, but live together under conditions of approximate social and economic equality, using in common the means that lie to their hands of promoting social welfare.

And two of the riders which Professor Cole added were:

a human fellowship which denies and expels distinctions of class, and a social system in which no one is so much richer or poorer than his neighbours as to be unable to mix with them on equal terms.

Not all the phrases in this passage are entirely unambiguous, but the general emphasis is clear—it is on the 'classless society'. As Professor Arthur Lewis has put it succinctly, 'Socialism is about equality'. And by equality is meant not simply equality of opportunity on the American model, but equality of status in the widest sense—subjective as well as objective.

Once accept this definition, and the differences between statism and socialism come sharply into focus. It is true that in the Britain of 1951 great strides towards equality had been made. Current incomes had been equalised to a quite remarkable extent, and opportunities also were more equal. But

61

Britain still did not begin to approach the ideal of a classless or egalitarian society. For all the redistribution of taxable income, there was still too great a spread in actual standards of life. The equalising intentions of fiscal policy could still be frustrated either by spending out of capital or by recourse to expense accounts, and they were widely frustrated in this way. The gap between the mode of life of the factory worker and of the regular *habitué* of the Four Hundred could scarcely be justified by socialist standards.

Much also remained to be done to equalise opportunities for entry to the professions and promotion in industry, and certainly no one could call Britain a society in which all had an equal chance.

But perhaps even more disturbing than this residue of objectively measurable social inequality was the persistence of a deep-seated *sense* of an unequal society. How deep this goes in Britain can be seen by a comparison with other countries whose actual degree of achieved equality is no greater (or is even less) than our own, but whose consciousness of equality and social solidarity is infinitely larger. To take two very different examples, both Sweden and the U.S.A. offer highly pertinent and disturbing comparisons in this respect.

Class feeling, and general social *malaise*, still persist in England to a deplorable extent. The feeling among workers of an eternal and irreconcilable conflict between wages and profits, capital and labour: their feeling too of non-participation in the control of the firm for which they work, and so of non-responsibility for its well-being: the acute sense of class that goes with different accents: the knowledge that differentials in education mean differentials in opportunity—these are all signs that Britain still is, and feels itself to be, a class society.

The purpose of socialism is quite simply to eradicate this sense of class, and to create in its place a sense of common interest and equal status. This will require not only more measures on the economic plane, directed to the greater equalisation of living standards and opportunities, but also measures on the socio-psychological plane. It is here that the essential difference between statism and socialism lies, and it is in this direction that socialists must look for the main advance.

If this point is accepted, we can at once dismiss certain lines of policy which are sometimes put forward as constituting the essence of good socialism.

(1) *The continued extension of free social services.* The redistribution of taxable income has now gone so far that any large new social services would fall to be paid for not by the rich, whose present untaxed income would be quite insufficient, but by the broad mass of the population—in other words, by the recipients of the new services. Thus no redistributive effect between rich and poor would be achieved. All that would happen would be that people were compelled, whether they liked it or not, to pay higher taxes on some sorts of goods in order to enjoy others free. This is not necessarily good. The object of social services is to provide a cushion of security against hardship due to unavoidable ill-fortune. Once the essential cushion has been provided, further advances in the national income should normally go to citizens in the form of 'free' income, to be spent as they wish, and not be taxed away and then returned in the form of some free service determined by the fiat of the state.

There are still, of course, many improvements which are urgently needed in the present social services. But socialists would be quite wrong to think that the essence of socialism lies in the indefinite extension of free services. A point will come when, unless a specific redistribution of income is desired (e.g. towards large families), the liberty of the citizen to spend his extra income as he pleases must also be regarded.

(2) *More and more nationalisation of whole industries.* Although the reaction against nationalisation has now gone too far, and the performance of the public sector has been very much better than is generally realised—far too little allowance is made for the fact that the industries chosen for nationalisation would have raised nearly insoluble problems in the post-war world under any form of ownership or control—yet it is clear that the further multiplication of public boards on the present model will not bring us rapidly nearer the socialist goal. Too many

problems remain to be solved in the existing nationalised industries, notably labour relations, decentralisation, and consumer control. The extension of public ownership will always remain an important auxiliary weapon, over the long run, for equalisation of gross income, since it substitutes fixed interest payments to capital for rising dividends. But its effects, in an economy already ruled by government controls and high taxation, are not enormous, and although the long-run case for it remains extremely strong it cannot, at least until existing problems are much nearer solution, be the main line of advance.

(3) *The continued proliferation of controls.* Controls over industry should be directed to certain basic planning ends—full employment, the balance of payments, location of industry, utility schemes, and the like. Beyond this they should not be multiplied (save in times of inflated demand, such as rearmament). A complex mass of detailed controls is highly unpopular, bad for industrial efficiency, and distorting in its effect on production. Within the framework of overall government planning, the proper way to make the private sector responsive to the needs of the community is to make it competitive. The failure to do so was perhaps the greatest single failure of the post-1945 Labour administration.

(4) *Further redistribution of income by direct taxation.* There has, over the last few years, been a great deal of bogy-talk about incentives. Most of this has been nonsense, and disproved by the actual output figures reached under a level of taxation that would have been considered fantastic a few years ago. Nevertheless, a limit must exist somewhere, and it is hard to believe that by 1951 the country was not very near that limit. In any event, the amount to be obtained by higher income taxation of the rich is quantitatively not significant, and would have no effect in making the poor less poor.

I do not mean that the final limit has necessarily been reached in any of these directions. No doubt further advances could be made in each of them. But I do mean that none of these four sets of policies, however popular or traditional, will take the country very much nearer socialism. It is in other directions that the left must turn for its new inspiration.

First, the ownership of wealth. The still gross maldistribution of property enables the upper classes, by spending out of capital, to live at a standard of luxury which their post-tax income would never alone permit. The degree of actual social inequality is thus much greater than the inequality of incomes, with corresponding results in respect of opportunity.

Secondly, the educational system. Nothing more amazes visitors from genuinely egalitarian countries (such as Sweden or New Zealand) than the existence in Britain of a social hierarchy of schools. Probably no other single factor is so influential in the propagation of class feeling.

Thirdly, the sphere of industry, whose right organisation constitutes the central problem of our time.

The crucial problem here is not that of social control. Those controls which are needed for planning purposes, and to correct the obvious deficiencies of a free price-mechanism, were already largely established under Labour rule (although they may require resuscitation after periods of Tory decontrol).

Nor is it the problem of consumer control, of ensuring that those goods are produced which the consumer most wants. This is a problem of creating sufficiently lively competition in the private sector; and in the nationalised sector of operating the correct price-rules under Ministerial and consumer council supervision.

Nor again is it mainly a problem of the distribution of the product. It is argued that shareholders, as the residuary legatees in industry, continuously earn a larger reward than is justified by the degree of risk involved. This may be so, but at present levels of taxation the point is not quantitatively important. The magnitudes involved are not such that great riches would accrue to the mass of the population from any reform, and the importance of this point lies really in the psychological field, and merges into the next question to be considered.

The crucial problem is the psychology of industrial relations, and the general tone and atmosphere in industry. Statism has provided negative economic satisfactions of the highest importance—full employment, high wages, security—and it has also strengthened the worker's bargaining position against his employer. But it has not given him a new social status, nor cured the basic class hostility which stems from his total exclusion from either rights or participation. Sole rights still belong to the functionless shareholder, and this knowledge still breeds frustration and annoyance among the workers.

Socialism requires that this hostility in industry should give way to a feeling of participation in a joint endeavour. How is this to be achieved? The most direct and easily exploitable line of advance is in the direction of joint consultation. Much fruitful work has been done in this sphere, and it is now clear that something more is needed than joint production committees on the present model—some more radical effort to give the worker a sense of participation in the making of decisions. A few progressive firms have already made bold advances, and the results are encouraging.

But this may not be enough as long as the workers know that the shareholders alone, though passive and (in the large firms) bearing little risk, have the only legal claim on a product which is jointly due to workers, managers and capital. Indeed, the legal framework of industry, considered logically or morally, is farcical in the contrast it presents between the sole ownership and rights of shareholders, and the essentially co-operative nature of the operations. If hostility to profits and dividends is not to bedevil industrial relations for all time, some resolution of this conflict must be found.

This question can only be solved by very radical measures, of which three suggest themselves. The first would be a large-scale extension of nationalisation. This eliminates the control of private owners, and reduces the return on capital to a fixed interest payment. Over the long run it must certainly be part of the answer—not so much for the traditional reasons (to facilitate planning, deal with monopolies, increase efficiency, etc.)—as in order gradually to substitute public rights for shareholders' rights, with beneficial effects both on the distribution of income and the psychology of industrial relations. But it would be foolish to pretend that this can provide a rapid solution while so many unsolved problems remain in the existing nationalised industries.

A second approach would be by statutory dividend limitation, not in the form of a rigid dividend 'freeze', but in some more flexible form (such as restricting dividends to a permitted percentage of total earnings, with exceptions for new or small businesses). This deserves much hard thought. Norwegian experience shows that it would not have the disastrous effects on enterprise that are sometimes prophesied, and it might play an important part in making a wages policy practicable. It would need to be accompanied by a new policy for undistributed profits. Since there would always be the chance of a Tory reaction, the large accumulation of company reserves might lead to a constant appreciation of share-values, which would partially frustrate the object of the scheme. Consideration must be given to the possibility of altering the legal ownership of company reserves, perhaps by the compulsory payment of bonus issues to the workers in the industry. A third possibility is so to alter the legal structure of company ownership as to substitute for shareholders' sole control a constitution which explicitly defines the responsibilities of the firm to worker, consumer and community; workers would become members of the company, and have their representatives on the board of directors. (This approach is discussed in more detail in a later essay.[1])

I do not pretend to know which of these lines of attack will turn out to be the right one. Far more thought and study is required. But I am certain that some unorthodox and revolutionary scheme is needed, even though its exact nature is not yet clear, if the workers—and they are the majority of the population—are to have a sense of partnership in, and responsibility for, the industry in which they work. And without this sense we shall remain a class society for all time.

Even a bare recital of these desiderata of socialism is enough to show what a long revolution still lies ahead. Statism cured

[1] See p. 121.

the worst social evils of the previous society, but its achievement was in a sense a negative one, confined to the elimination of abuses. It still remains to create the new society of which socialists have always dreamed, a society which is not bedevilled by the consciousness of class.

No one should think that this will be a short or an easy task. The easy and spectacular things have all been done, those that remain will need a prolonged and difficult effort of will. The pace will be limited, not only by the need to preserve the necessary minimum of social peace and cohesion, but also by the difficulty of engendering enthusiasm for further change in a population largely employed and enjoying rising standards every year. There will be no revival of the angry dynamic of revolt against the obvious miseries and injustices of capitalism. The temper of the people will be more contented and therefore more conservative, and public opinion will take time to acclimatise itself to the prospect of each further radical advance. These difficulties make it the more urgent that we should have a clear vision of where we want, as socialists, to go.

EQUALITY

Roy Jenkins

THE desire for greater equality has been part of the inspiration of all socialist thinkers and of all socialist movements. The absence of this desire, indeed, provides the most useful of all exclusive definitions of socialism. Where there is no egalitarianism there is no socialism.

The force and form of the desire have of course varied greatly. To take two seemingly extreme examples, Gracchus Babeuf was not only much shriller than Evan Durbin: he was also, thanks to his iconoclasm, his impossibilism and the violence of his times, much more urgent and absolute in his goal. But the direction was the same. And, indeed, the second example is not in reality an extreme one. For if we are looking for a stream of socialist thought in which the desire for equality has been weaker than elsewhere, it is not to a modern liberal socialist but to the Marxist-Leninists that we should turn. They have been more interested in capitalist maldistribution as a flaw to be used for the overthrow of the system than as an evil to be rectified for its own sake. They have been preoccupied with power relationships, and, uninterested in individuals, they have refused to believe that exploitation could take a form other than that of one economic class by another. As a result it is not surprising that Soviet Russia has less equality than any of the welfare states of the West, and less even than some of the more purely capitalist countries. Stalin cannot be strongly accused, in this respect, of betraying his intellectual masters.

British socialism, on the other hand, with its Christian inspiration and its debt to Benthamite radicalism, has always sought the equality of *individuals*. That this aim is central to Christian socialism is obvious; what is less obvious but equally true is that utilitarianism offered a basis for some of the simplest and most forceful of egalitarian arguments. Inequality was so

69

wasteful. It allowed increments of income, a twentieth part of which would have made all the difference between misery and comfort to a working-class family, to be received by the wealthy and spent or saved with equal indifference. As Shaw put it in the first of the original *Fabian Essays*: 'A New York lady, for instance, having a nature of exquisite sensibility, orders an elegant rosewood and silver coffin, upholstered in pink satin, for her dead dog. It is made: and meanwhile a live child is prowling barefooted and hunger-stunted in the frozen gutter outside. The exchange-value of the coffin is counted as part of the national wealth; but a nation which cannot afford food and clothing for its children cannot be allowed to pass as wealthy because it has provided a pretty coffin for a dead dog.'

A modicum of redistribution would obviously have increased the total welfare of the individuals who made up the nation. The liberal view that every individual had an equal right to seek his own happiness and the Marshallian concept of diminishing marginal utility, amounted, between them, to a very strong levelling case.

Why, in the nineteenth century, did it not have a greater effect upon those who were both liberals and believers in the classical economists? Partly because many, like Bentham himself, saw a conflict between liberty and equality, and gave a priority to the former; and partly, because, even if inequality was distributively wasteful, it could be argued that it was productively highly efficient. It created a saving class, who provided for a high level of investment and thus for a rapid expansion of the national income. If wealth had been evenly distributed, it would almost all have been consumed; and the theoretically possible remedy of state saving was too much at variance with the economic thought of the time to be practicable. Greater equality, it was thus suggested, could be bought only at the expense of a less dynamic economy.

Until 1914 this argument had much force. But thereafter, in the highly developed countries, capitalism began to stagnate, not for want of savings, but for want of investment opportunities. Inadequate consumption restricted investment to a level too low for full employment. The maximum use of resources and the rapid growth of national incomes began to demand not greater abstinence but increased consumption; and the key to this was a wider distribution of purchasing power. Inequality had lost its principal *raison d'être* and added a major item to its list of sins.

This development made the task of socialists who wished to do away with gross inequality somewhat easier. As the impact of the Keynesian analysis grew they were joined by the more intelligent of their opponents, who were willing to retreat from that degree of inequality which was incompatible with full employment and with the ability of capitalism to raise the standard of living. As a result, the superstructure of the welfare state has been imposed upon capitalism in this country, and to a lesser extent in the United States, without great difficulty.

No further help can be expected from this quarter. The degree of redistribution needed to make stagnating capitalism a system at once dynamic and tolerable, provided it was accompanied, as it has been, by measures of centralised planning, was not very great. In this country we have had at least enough, and probably a good deal more than enough, to serve this limited purpose. All those who became allies of equality not for its own sake, but because they realised it was necessary to make the system work, are now back on the other side.

But their defection has not destroyed any of the traditional socialist case for equality. This was not based on a Keynesian analysis of the productive inefficiency of gross inequality. Socialists have always hated the injustice of inequality for its own sake, because they agreed with Colonel Rainborough of Cromwell's army that 'the poorest he that is in England hath a life to live as the greatest he'; because they have been convinced that the more evenly wealth is divided the more welfare it will promote; and because they have believed that while no system of distribution will exactly equate reward with service, a nearly equal one comes much nearer to so doing than does a grossly unequal one.

This case is intact to-day, and even if no longer reinforced by the special arguments of the slump years, is far stronger than it was before 1914, because the big saver is no longer of any economic importance. It is central to any socialist approach and it is certainly one of the things which politics in this country, for many decades to come, will be about. A straightforward struggle between the capitalists and the proletariat for power over the productive machinery of the nation, in the Marxist sense, there will not be. The capitalists have already surrendered too much power, partly to the state, partly to their own managers, and partly to the trade unions, for a determined stand to be practicable. A classical Marxist clash is not possible in a situation in which, before it takes place, the President of the National Union of Mineworkers is already more powerful than any six capitalists. What will be at issue is, in the first place, whether the capitalists, having surrendered or had taken from them so much of their power, and therefore of their functions, should be allowed to retain the quite substantial portion of their privileges which still remain to them; and, in the second place, whether the society which is growing out of capitalism is to be a participant, democratic socialist society, or whether it is to be a managerial society, controlled by a privileged elite enjoying a standard of living substantially different from that of the mass of the population.

The whole of the former struggle, and much of the more important latter one, the outcome of which is far from certain, will be played out in the form of a dispute over the distribution of the national income. What should be the aim of those who, in this struggle, are for more equality? A definition in mathematical terms is impracticable. What can be said is that the degree of equality to be sought should provide the economic framework for a classless society. And a classless society can be defined, quite simply, as one in which men will be separated from each other less sharply by variations in wealth and origin than by differences in character. Such a society will certainly not be monolithic, for its establishment will in no way depend upon the obliteration of the many true and desirable differences between human beings. Indeed, these distinctions will be the more obvious and the more developed as they become less obscured by artificial differences of wealth and class.

There is no need to decry the great advances towards equality which have been made in the past twelve years, in order to make clear how far we are still from the attainment of such a society. Redistribution has narrowed the gap not only by reducing the living standards of the wealthy, but also, a very much more difficult thing to achieve, by raising those of the poor. But it has stopped short at a point at which 1% of the population still has nearly 50% of the nation's capital wealth; at which there are still over 400 persons owning more than a million pounds' worth of property; at which there are still about 2,100 persons with gross incomes of more than £20,000 a year (60% of these incomes being less than a half earned, and nearly 40% of them wholly unearned); and at which, even after the present heavy rates of direct taxation, the largest net incomes are still more than thirty times the smallest adult wage.

Therefore, even if we cannot yet see the exact shape of the goal, the direction in which we must move is perfectly clear. What should be the pace and methods of advance? In practice, it must first be said, the pace is far more likely to be too slow rather than too fast. The British people, in the past, have enjoyed their periods of rapid social advance in small doses and at infrequent if remarkably regular intervals. The pattern formed by the dates 1830, 1868, 1906 and 1945 does not suggest that strong left-wing governments, backed by heavy parliamentary majorities and filled with reforming zeal, necessarily follow each other very quickly. In the future there may be the added difficulty that great numbers of people will consider welfare capitalism a comfortable and stable form of society and will be in no hurry to change it; and this may apply with special force to the question of equality, for, in an increasingly 'bourgeoisiefied' society, so many will believe themselves to be on the wrong side of the line around which further measures of redistribution will take place. Any egalitarian who believes that, in this country, the forces of history are working inexorably towards his goal is living in a fool's paradise. It may be even more difficult to make a little further progress in this direction than is the case in most other fields of social endeavour.

It must therefore be recognised, that the difficulties are likely to be such that socialists need devote little thought to the fear that the pace of advance may be too rapid. There will be plenty of other people to see that this is not so. At the same time it should be acknowledged, and kept as a thought at the back of our minds, that a cataclysmic advance towards almost complete equality, even if it were practicable, would be self-defeating.

A classless society will demand a far more co-operative form of living than we now have. The change of nature which this will require will certainly not occur overnight, and until this change has largely occurred, it may well be safer to allow many individuals to seek, within a controlled framework, for monetary distinction, rather than to channel away their desires in more harmful directions. Furthermore, the evolution of stronger non-monetary incentives, while it is by no means an impossible task, is likely to be a rather slow one. A classless society does not of course demand a reliance on them alone—differences in reward for variations in effort and skill, such as now exist between members of the same household, obviously do not of themselves create a distinction of class—but it clearly does imply that they shall become of much greater relative importance. And until non-monetary incentives are able more effectively to fulfil this role, the needs of rising production, which this country must have—partly because of the settled expectation of a rising standard of living which its people now possess, and partly because of the contribution which it must make, even if we are actuated by no motives higher than those of long-term self-interest, to raising the standards of living of other peoples—demand a certain caution.

There is also the point that great changes must be made within a framework of widespread consent, both because it would be wrong in itself to do otherwise, and because, unless they are so made and if the object is to create a more democratic order of society, they will defeat their own ends. A sudden move to destroy all existing inequalities of wealth and income, which offended a settled view of the majority of the people, would have as its almost inevitable result the creation of a new class of undemocratic power-holders, who would quickly attain to the status of a material elite from which, just because of the concentrated and undemocratic nature of their power, they might be more difficult to remove than are the existing possessors of privilege. Only those who accept the dangerous Marxist utopianism of regarding the end of capitalist exploitation not as a prerequisite of a classless society but as in itself a certain guarantee and a full definition of such a society, can regard this danger with equanimity.

Therefore, recognising that it is the duty of socialists to press as hard as they can for an ever greater degree of equality, but accepting the fact that such delays as will occur should not, for the reasons just given, be treated with too much intolerance, we can turn to the methods of advance.

First, we have the methods which have been used in the past. The recent move towards equality can be largely accounted for under the two heads of the change from mass unemployment to full employment and of the use of heavy taxation upon the rich to finance a greatly extended structure of social services. The former change has not only enabled a great number of persons who were previously below the poverty level to earn a reasonable wage; it has also substantially improved the bargaining position of the whole wage-earning class, and therefore the pre-tax share of the national income which its members have been able to obtain. But it is not a weapon which remains sharp for use. Transition towards full employment cannot be a continuous process.

The latter weapon is also at least partially exhausted. Rates of taxation upon income, while they might certainly be marginally increased, particularly in the case of the middle ranges of surtax, could not be made to yield any further appreciable sum which would be available for re-distribution (the obliteration of net incomes of more than £2,000 would bring the Exchequer only £60 million a year); and the position of the very rich could not be further attacked by this means without resort to the extreme disincentive of a 100% tax on very high incomes.

It follows that any further extensions in the social services which take place (defining an extension as an increase in the percentage of the national income devoted to the service) are unlikely to be redistributive in any broad class sense. They may be redistributive between the unmarried sheet-metal worker and the railwayman with a wife and children, or between all those within the wage-earning age bracket and the old age pensioners; and these changes may in themselves be very necessary and desirable, but they will not affect the class structure. Advances here must therefore be viewed with caution. The working class is already paying for a large part of the social services which it enjoys, and this will be still more the case with any further extensions which take place. Such extensions may do much more to restrict liberty than to promote equality, for they may merely transfer from the individual to the state the decision as to how that individual is to dispose of a given amount of purchasing power; and such a development, in the absence of the strongest and most specific of social cases in its favour, should be viewed by democratic socialists with grave suspicion.

In any case, even if it were not for the serious practical difficulties in the way, we have already made do long enough with various makeshift devices to combat, often but not always successfully, a thoroughly intolerable and unjustifiable distribution of income at source. Both the exhaustion of our 'devices' and their inherent illogicality, demand that we should now try to get nearer to the root of the matter.

This involves three things: the stiffer taxation of property, an enlarged field of public ownership, and a complete freedom of entry, subject only to the possession of the necessary skill or ability, into all occupations.

Measures of property taxation (whether by means of a levy or by means of greatly increased death duties) are similar to further measures of income taxation in that they would not make available any great sum for redistribution to the less well-off: huge sums might be raised by the state by means of a levy, but capital cannot be spent as income without having a strong inflationary effect. But they are unlike them in that they would not run us sharply up against the problem of incentives. The removal by the state of a large part of the reward which a man gets for working must always be a factor tending against effort, although, as it may well be cancelled by equally more powerful factors making in the other direction, it certainly cannot be assumed that high taxation and low production must go hand in hand. The expropriation by the state of a large part of the store of wealth which a man has received, either through no effort on his own part or through effort long past and quite disproportionately highly rewarded at the time, is very different. Such expropriation may well make a man work, not less hard, but harder.

Capital taxation is also unlike income taxation in that it is an attack at the roots of inequality and not at its surface manifestations. It does not temporarily reduce the value of a large unearned income; it destroys it permanently. In this way it is an effective and indispensable way of dealing with the anachronistic privileges of the now increasingly functionless *owning* class, and must play a large part in the fiscal policies of future Labour Governments.

There are three principal forms which a fiscal attack upon property might take: a capital gains tax, the stepping up of death duties, and a capital levy. The first is at present the most canvassed. It is obviously practicable, having been in operation in the United States for the past quarter of a century; it would attack a form of profit-making which draws attention to itself and is therefore a good deal resented, and it enjoys the distinction of having been one of the few clear-cut suggestions in the Labour Party's manifesto at the last election. For these and other reasons such a tax has much to commend it. But it would be fatal to think of it as the principal fiscal tool for the promotion of greater capital equality. Its first limitation is that it can do nothing to reduce existing stores of wealth; it can only moderate the speed at which they can be increased. And American experience does not suggest that it is necessarily very effective here. Of course, it can be argued that the rates of tax in this country could be much stiffer than those which have been applied in the United States. But such a stiffening would bring us up against two further difficulties. The first is that, the stiffer the rates, the more accurate a method of assessment becomes necessary, and a highly accurate method of assessment, demanding a continual series of property valuations, would place upon the revenue authorities a burden of work quite disproportionate to the results which would follow. The second difficulty is that a rate of tax which took away almost the whole of a capital gain would make the investment of money in risky enterprises very much less attractive than has hitherto been the case. Even with very high rates of surtax the prospect of capital appreciation has provided a substantial inducement to risk-taking.

This is the major objection to a very heavy tax on capital gains. A continuing tax upon recently acquired capital, it would have far more disincentive effect than almost any other form of property taxation; and it would hit the active capitalist as opposed to the established proprietor who lacked either the will or the ability to add to his fortune. This is not an argument against using a moderate scale of tax to add to the revenue (although the yield, except in periods of sharp inflation, could easily be exaggerated) and to extract some contribution from the speculator. It is an argument against pushing the scale too high or trying to make a tax which hits only one form of wealth, and that not necessarily the least desirable, accomplish too much.

The death duties are not open to these objections. They are not markedly disincentive, they hit all forms of wealth equally, and they are certainly able, over a period, substantially to deplete existing stores of wealth. And there is more room for a stiffening of the rates than is generally thought to be the case. The Finance Acts of 1946 and 1949 made the scales much more progressive, and estates of £1,000,000 or more now attract duty at the rate of 80%. These scales have not been in operation nearly long enough for it to be possible to say how rapid a re-distribution of property they are producing, or to what extent the effect is offset by the re-growth of individual fortunes during an average lifetime. It is, however, worth remembering that the redistributive effects of death duties in the past have been much less dramatic than it was expected that they would be.

In any event, the death duties, even at their existing rates, are not sufficiently stiff to destroy large unearned incomes within a generation. A gross fortune of £10,000,000 will pass as £2,000,000, giving an income of about £80,000 a year, and one of £200,000 will pass as £90,000, giving an income of about £3,600 a year. To carry the argument a stage further, a £10,000,000 fortune could pass through to the fifth generation, without making any allowance for the creation of new wealth by any of the heirs, or even for the secular tendency of certain forms of property to rise in value, before it became so reduced as to be unlikely to produce an income of £2,000 a year; another two generations would receive incomes of more than £1,000. In the case of a fortune of £200,000, three generations of heirs could hope for unearned incomes of £2,000 a year or more, and five generations for incomes of £1,000 a year or more.

If, therefore, it is proposed to use death duties, not merely to moderate inherited wealth, but, at least in so far as it gives rise to unearned incomes big enough to support people in whole lifetimes of idleness, to destroy it, they must be stepped up. An effective limit to the size of fortunes which it was thought desirable should pass might be fixed—the figure could not be much below £25,000 without giving rise to all sorts of complications with widows and others unable to support themselves, and not much above if all are to work, at some stage in their lives, for their main support—and fortunes above that figure might be made subject to 95% or even 100% duty. Fortunes below that figure might well be exempted entirely from duty.

Such a scheme would be open to two objections. It would be slow in its effects, for the average frequency with which fortunes change hands is once in thirty years; and during this transitional period the rich would have the strongest of incentives to dispose of their property above the exemption figure.

They might do so by a great increase in gifts *inter vivos*, which would destroy the purpose of the stiffened death duties, or, if the Inland Revenue authorities closed this loophole, they might do so by a greatly accelerated spending of capital, so that the new duties would only be effective at the expense of thirty years of very high spending by the rich, and of a greater inequality of living standards during this period than exists to-day.

This difficulty arises inevitably from the fact that death duties on the scale suggested are nothing more than a very severe capital levy, with those who are to be hit getting several decades' notice that they are the target. The only way to avoid this is to make the tax a capital levy in name as well as in fact and to impose it with as little notice as possible. But the levy would need to be on just as stringent a scale as the rates of death duty suggested if it were to achieve the primary purpose of destroying all fortunes big enough to yield really large unearned incomes. And, if the problem of notice were to be solved, it would have to be imposed at one blow rather than in a series of small attacks. A heavy levy which was obviously a prelude to a still heavier one in a few years' time would be just as likely to lead to a dissipation of capital as would a further stiffening of the death duties.

Here, then, is a dilemma. Great fortunes (and with them great unearned incomes) can only be ended, without provoking an avalanche of capital spending, by means of a sudden blow. Is such a blow compatible with progress within a framework of consent? It is not an easy question to answer. Certainly such a complete overturning of existing property relationships should only be undertaken by a strong government which had placed its views on the subject, in general terms, fairly before the electorate. Even then there would be advantages in moderating the impact of the levy, without destroying its essential purpose, so far as this could be done. The suggestion which offers itself is that of the state continuing to pay a part of the income from the surrendered property to its previous owner for either a lifetime or a fixed number of years. Such an arrangement would combine the more gradual approach of the death duty method with the adequate guarantee that capital would not be dissipated which is the great attraction of the sudden and heavy levy method.

Our next weapon is more public ownership. This is closely related to the taxation of great fortunes—for it is idle to postulate an economy in which 70–80% of the enterprises remain under private ownership, unless it is proposed to leave in existence the private aggregations of wealth which alone make such owner-ship possible—but it also offers a means by which a greater equality of earned incomes, before tax, may be promoted. Many egalitarians would to-day say that they were disillusioned with nationalisation. By paying generous scales of compen-sation, they would argue, the possibility of using it as a means of promoting a greater equality of property had been lost, and by paying high salaries to the members of public boards, and to a lesser extent to their subordinates, the possibility of using it as a means of promoting a greater equality of income had also been lost.

The first argument is hardly a serious one. Partial nationalisa-tion, unless the state were to behave quite irrationally, necessarily involved compensation; there was no possible justification for expropriating the owners of the railways, rich and not so rich, merely because they were railway share-holders, and leaving the fortunes of cotton-owners unscathed. Wholesale nationalisation, while it would not have been com-patible with political democracy, would at least have escaped this difficulty. It, and it alone, would have made confiscation a logically defensible policy. The third alternative was that of paying inadequate compensation—that is to say, compensation mixed up with an element of confiscation. But to have penalised certain persons for having invested in an industry which was one of the Labour Party's candidates for nationalisation, while not penalising them enough to destroy their privileged position, would have had nothing to be said for it.

In any event, too many sins should not be laid at the door of the compensation policy which has been pursued. While it did not penalise the individual shareholder, for it gave him a gilt-edged security equal in value, at the date of transfer, to the equity which he had lost (and which he could quickly re-exchange for another equity if he so wished), it did exclude the private investor as a class from the future profits of the industry which had been taken over. In a period of gradual decline in the value of money, which is probably an inevitable con-comitant of full employment in a mixed economy, this is a consideration of some importance. The prices of steel shares would have been rising rapidly in 1951 had it not been for nationalisation; the fixed-interest securities for which they were exchanged did not react in the same way.

This factor apart, however, public ownership in this context is important not because it creates a greater equality of wealth, but because it must follow from the creation of a greater equality by other means.

The second argument against nationalisation, as a policy making for greater equality, rests on the high salaries paid to members of public undertakings. This argument has some force (although, at the highest levels at any rate, public salaries are substantially lower than those which would be paid for jobs of equal responsibility in private industry), but it only makes sense if it is accompanied by a demand for more public ownership. A 20% public sector cannot hope to set the salary standard for the whole of industry. It can either make itself a small island of low rewards (rather as the Co-operative Movement has done), and probably pay for this by a low standard of managerial efficiency, or it can tag along behind the private sector, offering rather lower salaries, but not so much lower as, with the present rates of surtax, seriously to affect its recruiting ability. Of these two alternatives the latter, which has been chosen, is probably slightly preferable, but no one can argue that the choice is very inspiring, or that either course is a satis-factory long-term solution.

If, on the other hand, public concerns were in a position to set the standard for the rest of industry, the situation would be very different. The ratio between the highest and the lowest payments within a nationalised industry could be greatly narrowed, and not only would there be no loss of talent to concerns which remained under private ownership, but the effect of such a move would be more widespread because of the leadership which the public sector was able to exercise. In this way additional public control over the difference between the standard of living of the managerial class and that of the rest of the community could be established. A highly privileged elite could still emerge, but if it did the rest of the community would have only itself and its elected representatives to blame.

How big a public sector would be necessary before this leadership could be exercised? No precise answer can be given, although, as a very rough and indirect guide, monopolistic concerns are generally assumed to be able to exercise price leadership when they control 40% of the market. But, whatever may be the answer, whether it be 40% or 60% or 80%, socialist aims in this field cannot possibly be regarded as fulfilled until the figure has been reached.

A substantial extension of public ownership is thus an essential prerequisite of greater equality of earned incomes and an inevitable concomitant of greater equality in the ownership of property. But the form of public ownership need not follow existing patterns. The measures of nationalisation which we saw between 1945 and 1950 were largely *planning* measures. They were put forward as proposals which were necessary to ensure adequate governmental control over the whole economy, and the industries which were chosen were mostly those through which this function could best be exercised. As a result, they were necessarily measures which involved whole industries and which imposed a centralised structure upon them. All the main line railway companies had to be taken and it would not have done to have substituted catering for coal.

Beyond steel the position becomes different. Transfers to public ownership in the future may in part be anti-monopoly measures, and may in part be efficiency measures, but they will be primarily egalitarian measures, and they will hardly be planning measures at all. It should consequently be possible to break away from the association of public ownership with a highly centralised organisation and to seek more intimate forms of ownership and control. Industries need not be taken over as a whole, and part ownership of particular firms may even be a satisfactory solution in certain circumstances. More important still, public ownership need not mean state ownership. The local authorities, consumers' and producers' co-operatives, and other public bodies must be encouraged to play a full part in the ownership of enterprises. The essentials to be achieved are that a pattern of ownership compatible with the abolition of great fortunes should be worked out, and that control over the rewards of the managers should be firmly in the hands of those whose natural interests are opposed to privilege, except in so far as such privilege is strictly necessary to the success of the economy; and these essentials are in no way incompatible with a high degree of decentralisation.

The third weapon is the attainment of full freedom of entry into all occupations. This is largely a matter of equality of educational opportunity, including equal opportunity to train for and enter professions involving expensive post-graduate study or an initial period of very low earnings; but it is also a matter of ending, so far as possible, the power of nepotic appointment. This is at present most exercised in medium and small-scale industry and in the City of London. It is a function of the concentration of ownership in a comparatively small number of hands and of the present outdated legal position, which makes management solely responsible to the stockholders. It is not suggested that the nepotic element in all appointments, either in public or in private concerns, can ever be completely eradicated, but a retreat from these two conditions would make it increasingly difficult for it to be the principal element.

The attainment of complete freedom of entry into all occupations should bring to an end, over a period, the attachment of 'monopoly revenue' to the possession of certain qualifications, except in so far as the monopoly lies in the possession of

inherent ability. Payment for time spent in acquiring special
knowledge and skills there must continue to be, but it should
be related to the real sacrifice of time and effort involved
in such acquisition, and not to the traditional right of those
who have acquired the qualifications to a much higher
standard of living than other people. This means, not only that
there should be no class restriction on entry into highly qualified
occupations, but that there should be no rigid bureaucratically
imposed numerical restriction either. If lawyers or engineers
are sufficently scarce that they are able to earn incomes greatly
in excess of the average, other people should be free to correct
the balance by swelling their numbers until their rewards fall to
a more reasonable level. For this to happen it is necessary that
those with high technical or professional qualifications should
not exercise too much control over the general shape of the
economy and of society, but that their power should be constantly modified by that of those who have no managerial
pretensions. If this is not so, the results of equal opportunity may
be good in that they ensure the full use of the talent that is
available, but disappointing as a contribution to greater
equality.

Equal opportunity is therefore in itself no guarantee of full
equality, and there would be certain dangers in concentrating
too much attention upon it without ensuring that it was accompanied by other egalitarian measures such as those already
mentioned. A society insisting upon complete equality of
opportunity, but allowing or encouraging great differences in
living standards and a low degree of participation in affairs by
the mass of the population, might be more efficient and more
permanent, but less desirable, than one which combined the
survival of a fair degree of nepotism and hereditary status with
a climate of opinion favourable to greater material equality. The
former would not be a classless society, because the working class
would still be sharply divided from those in control, by wealth
and power, if not by heredity or tradition, but it would be a
society in which ability and leadership were closely concentrated
at the top. The working class would be stripped of its talent in a

way that has never before been the case, and it would be difficult either for a movement which challenged the existing order of things, and particularly the existing distribution of wealth, to become effective, or for the workers to secure and exercise a greater voice in the control of industry. Had there been complete equality of opportunity and no social rigidity in the England of 1900, it is probable both that the Labour Movement in its present form would never have existed and that the gap between the standards of living of those who remained manual workers and those who acquired other jobs would be much greater to-day than is actually the case.

To some extent, of course, these difficulties are already present in our society. The 'working-class' leadership of the Labour Party is not as strong as it was a few decades ago, and this weakness may be expected to become more acute as the present degree of freedom of entry to the universities works itself out fully, and those who, had they been born in an earlier generation, might have become Hendersons or Bevins, are drained off to be turned into 'middle-class intellectuals'. They may return to play a part in the political leadership of the working class, but they will be unable to do much on the industrial side, and, in any event, their natural authority will be less than that of those who came to leadership through a more strictly indigenous process.

In the same way untapped reserves of leadership and ability are probably becoming increasingly rare amongst groups of unskilled workers. It thus becomes more difficult to throw a problem to a gang of men and ask them both to provide the answer and do the job. The man who, some time ago, would have provided the leadership may now have been creamed off to act either in a managerial or a representative capacity. It may, in some ways, be easier to hand over the management of a factory to its workers in a new industrial country like Yugoslavia, where there has been little opportunity for the proletariat to acquire new skills and to rise in the occupational scale, than in an old one like Britain, where the process of 'creaming-off' has been going on for some time.

Equality of opportunity is an important and useful weapon, but one to be handled with some caution. It should be used only in association with other weapons making for greater equality of reward and for more parity of esteem between those receiving different rewards. Otherwise it will produce a more productively efficient economy only at the expense of a less cohesive, less participant and less reformable society. If the advances towards equality of opportunity which have so far taken place in Great Britain have not produced these results (except in so far as any move away from a rigidly hierarchical order of things is thought to involve less social cohesion), it is because they have done no more than keep in step with other egalitarian advances, notably the scaling down of income differences, the decline in respect for wealth as such, and the growth of respect for the claims on society of the unsuccessful as well as the successful. The United States, on the other hand, has been as much ahead of this country in equality of opportunity as it has been behind in other facets of progress towards equality, and the resultant disparity has produced at least some of the evils which might have been expected. A restlessly competitive society, a greater respect for money than in more traditional countries, and a social climate in which it has been difficult for a radical movement to take firm root have all been features of the American scene. Only those who would welcome such developments in this country should regard equal opportunity as *in itself* an answer. To do so is certainly not good socialism. It is not even good Toryism. It is nothing but nineteenth-century liberalism.

This essay has continually emphasised both that one of the principal objects of greater equality should be the creation of a more democratic society with a wider diffusion of power, and that an essential condition for the maintenance of equality once it has been achieved is the existence of a vigorous participant democracy. It is easy to see how greater equality of reward, more general access to higher educational facilities, and an improvement in the status of the manual worker might assist the growth of democracy in industry and encourage people of all sorts to play a more active part in the work and control of public and voluntary organisations. What is perhaps more difficult is to envisage the future of democracy in its strictly political aspects in a largely egalitarian society.

In the English political tradition liberty and equality have certainly not been automatically interchangeable words. The power of the individual, as opposed to that of the state, and his freedom to stand aside from or actively to oppose the dominant political beliefs of the day, without any loss of rights, are essentially products of the Whig revolution. And one of the inevitable results of the transition to an egalitarian society would be the destruction of such vestiges of Whiggery, in the sense of a system of limited liberty based upon the ability of the great magnate to defy the central power, as still remain. Would this lead to a loss of political liberty? Obviously there are ways in which it is easier to tyrannise over a society of equals, in which nobody enjoys prestige or power except in so far as he earns it by his contribution to society (the value of which must be judged by those who at the time exercise the dominating influence), than over a society in which certain individuals enjoy undeserved but almost inalienable hereditary rights of wealth or influence. Equally obviously, a society which destroys these privileges and yet escapes tyranny will have achieved a more complete freedom than one which can only defend liberty by restricting many of its benefits to a few. How high the sights should be set must depend upon the stage of development of the particular society. The fact that Whiggery was necessary to the creation of English political liberty in the seventeenth and eighteenth centuries does not mean that it is necessary to its maintenance in the second half of the twentieth century. Indeed, in so far as the social and economic inadequacies of liberalism may be regarded as the most powerful of the influences which have caused men, in the first half of this century, voluntarily to abandon their political liberties, Whiggery may now be thought of as at least as powerful a creator of the forces of tyranny as it is an obstacle to their effectiveness. Nevertheless, it will be well to guard against the removal of its protection by ensuring that our new society of near equals is left confronting a state machine in which power, both economic and political, is as widely diffused as possible. This is one reason why, as has already been suggested, the ownership of enterprises, when it passes from wealthy individuals, should go, not to the state, but to less remote public bodies.

The party system, which is and has been so much the essence of British political democracy that it is difficult to believe that it is not a *sine qua non*, may also be thought to be endangered by a substantial move towards egalitarianism. Must not the one-class state also be the one-party state? Certainly the rigid Marxist, to whom this development would not in any event appear a very dreadful calamity, would have to answer the question with a clear affirmative. And even those who are a good deal less rigid but who none the less believe in the dominance of the economic motive as a spring to political action, could only escape from such an answer by postulating a new party grouping arising out of conflicts between those in one productive or geographical group and those in another—not a very likely development in a country so closely integrated and so impregnated by a common tradition as the United Kingdom.

A more realistic answer is that the move towards and even the attainment of a classless society might well leave largely undisturbed the present party basis. Certainly the immensely resilient Conservative Party, which has survived so skilfully the social changes of the past 150 years, would not collapse under the disappearance of the *bourgeoisie*. There is always room in British politics for a party of consolidation, and provided there are leaders prepared to play the role of a Sir Robert Peel or a Mr. R. A. Butler, and ensure that it is merely no advance and not positive reaction which is attempted, the future of conservatism is assured. Its basis of support is not only or even principally those who feel that their economic class interests would be endangered by the reformers. It comes from the much more numerous class of those who, without particular regard for their own economic interests, shrink from the intellectual adventure of supporting a government of advance. They are the sceptics, the pessimists about man's ability to improve his own lot, who reject not so much this or that aspect of the reforming party's programme as the whole concept that changes wrought by government can make a better society. They will always exist, and in great numbers, in a classless society as much as in a hierarchical one, and they will always offer a solid basis of support for a party of the right.

It is the position of the party of the left which would be more in doubt as the approach to a classless society became closer. A reforming party is always in danger of destroying itself by its own success. By a policy of removing inequalities, it opens itself wide to this danger, for the further the process is pushed the fewer there will be who will stand to benefit, in a material sense, from any further advance. But just as it would be inadequate to analyse the basis of support of the Conservative Party in terms of those who stand materially to lose by change, so it would be equally inadequate to analyse that of the Labour Party in terms of those who stand to gain. There will always be, to counter the pessimists of the right, the optimists of the left, those who believe that a better society is round the corner and that it can be attained by human will and human effort. They are perpetual reformers, and the first duty of the party of the left is to remain true to their faith and to command their loyalty: to be radical in the context of the moment. To-day that demands a high degree of priority for further measures of equalisation. But when the aims in this field come near to fulfilment, there will be others which will open up and provide an adequate basis of support for a reforming party which remains open-minded and undazzled by its own success.

EDUCATION AND SOCIAL DEMOCRACY
Margaret Cole

WHEN the plan for this book was being discussed, a Fabian who had heard something of its prospective contents commented, 'Why a chapter on education rather than on any other of the social services?' This question, in that form, could scarcely have been put in any country other than England; it chimes in with the parallel question, 'Why are educational conferences so fearfully dull?' and shows quite clearly the many difficulties in the way of making an educational policy—to say nothing of a socialist educational policy—for this country.

Educational conferences are very often dull. But the main reason for this is not, as is sometimes said, that those who take part in them pontificate or talk officialese. Educators do, of course, do both—maybe to a slightly greater extent, owing to the nature of their profession, than those in other walks of life— but many who are not headmasters pontificate, and the use of administrative jargon is not confined to education officers or inspectors. The main reason is that the 'education' which is their nominal subject has had, since the Age of Enlightenment, two essentially different ideals—education as a preparation for life (including real vocational education), and public instruction for the prevention of nuisance. To try to discuss these two ideas under a single blanket heading is simply to invite confusion and platitude.

The past history of 'education' in England is of course well-known in its broad lines—the continued co-existence of two systems, the private or endowed and the state system, which, however much they have been modified, have influenced each other, or become blurred at the edges, still make up the essential picture of to-day. 'One education for the rich and another for the poor' has long been a commonplace. But though this phrase was literally true during the whole of the nineteenth

91

century, and though it is very largely true to-day, when the results of past parsimony hang as a burden of infinite weight around the necks of *all* local education authorities, it is too purely economic adequately to express the state of things. It is not merely standards of pay and qualifications of teachers; it is not merely huge classes and horrible buildings; it is the underlying attitude of mind which so divides the two systems, which keeps the public school educator so abysmally ignorant of the barest facts about the great bulk of state education, and the state educator so irritated at the airy Utopianism or fearful exclusiveness of his counterpart in the private sector.

Obviously, it is the first idea—education as a preparation for life—that must be the idea of socialists and democrats. It has, in fact, always been the idea, not merely of educational theorists from Plato to Stalin, but of every parent who was consciously concerned for the upbringing of his children. This does not mean, it should be observed, that the education so planned has always been either a good thing in itself, or even happily devised for the end it was seeking to achieve; that depends in the one case upon the sort of life for which you think it desirable to prepare, and in the second on your competence to choose rightly. Few socialists, notwithstanding the special pleading of the High Master of Manchester Grammar School, believe the Platonic system of education to be democratic in its purpose; and, to take a more glaring example, the Nazi ideal of what life should be produced a consciously controlled educational system, that described in *School for Barbarians*, which was vile.

These are two instances of systems planned to prepare for a way of life which socialism rejects: under the heading of wrong or misguided choice one could cite freely. For example, it is scarcely credible that anyone could believe that the institution of Long Chamber at Eton, as it was in the first forty years of last century, or the confining of the studies of first-form boys for a whole year to Latin grammar and accidence and nothing else whatever, could be an adequate preparation for the life of a male member of the governing classes; yet it took two generations—such is the pace of educational reform even when there is no question of rates or taxes involved—before a handful of determined headmasters succeeded in putting an end to that regime. In the other system, we see the Special Place examination in this century, belying the intentions of its devisers and becoming the most furiously contested educational struggle in the country, because the good parent of the primary school child believed fervently that to get into a grammar school, no matter what the pabulum provided therein, was in virtue of its social standing a better preparation for life than any other his child could receive. It is no use blaming parents for this, or accusing them of snobbery, or wailing that there are to-day children in grammar schools who ought not to be there, because a largely bookish curriculum does not suit them. There are such cases, though probably not so many as the Cassandras make out; these are the 'premature leavers' who are taken away not so much because their parents cannot afford to keep them there— there is a good deal of nonsense talked about the temptation of the child's earnings—but because 'We don't see what good it's doing him'. But so long as, in an unequal society, having been at a 'better' school is, or is believed to be, a valuable preparation for life, so long shall we find children getting in, or struggling to get in, to schools which are not the right sort of schools for them. It is certainly no answer to try and keep them from falling out again by poking bits of inadequate technical and commercial education into grammar schools whose rolls are falling.

I shall return later in this essay to the problem of the purposes of education in the mid-twentieth century and how they are to be achieved. But I must note in passing that Labour policy on education seems never really to have faced this question of dual purpose in present-day society, but to have contented itself with vague though well-enough-justified indignation about 'privilege'. Even Tawney's eloquent plea of 1922, *Secondary Education for All*, contains little more than its title suggests; it is a cry for justice for the deprived; it does not ask what kind of secondary education or for what ends; and where, in later years, Labour has been able to influence the course of educational development, it has betrayed again and again that it does not know whether by 'secondary education for all' it means 'equal attention paid to the secondary education of children of all types' or 'equal opportunity for everybody to go to a public school'. Quite often Labour councillors and Labour voters have seemed unaware that there is any clash between these two interpretations.

Meanwhile, we have with us the appalling heritage of the second ideal—public instruction as a prevention of public nuisance. It would be easy, and is very tempting, to write at length on the shameful story of English public education down to the Act of 1902; even to re-read it makes one's blood boil in the good old-fashioned way. It is only necessary here, however, to recall the highlights, or deepest glooms.

It was a 'prevention of nuisance' service from the outset, from the day when Robert Raikes began to demonstrate to the citizens of Gloucester that Sunday in Gloucester was a much more decorous and comparatively pleasurable day when the wild hooligan children, the *bezprizhorni* of our Industrial Revolution, were shut up for the day in Sunday Schools; the most potent argument used to convert the non-converted to the need for charitable and state contributions to the cost of schooling was the pure one of public hygiene, of keeping the children out of the streets and preventing pilfering[1]—and schools were cheaper than reformatories and prisons. A little later, when Joseph Lancaster produced triumphant calculations to show that through the monitorial system 200 children could be instructed in the elements for the sum of 1*d.* per head per week, this enchanting discovery enabled the philanthropic to add to the prevention of public nuisance the prevention of the nuisance of the illiterate who could not read the Bible or sign their names. It is fairly often stated that the elimination of illiteracy was essential for a growing industrial society, but this does not seem

[1] Exactly the same argument as is used to-day by those collecting subscriptions for youth clubs in 'tough' areas. The disquieting experiences of early war-time, when the evacuation muddle left hundreds of thousands of children at large in the big cities, showed clearly enough that this argument still holds: state education is still essential to elementary civilisation. But this is not now its main purpose even in the minds of magistrates.

to be historical fact until the 'sixties, at least, when Robert Lowe seriously observed 'we must at least persuade our future masters to learn their letters'.[1] In the earlier decades Lancaster was regarded as a philanthropist and illuminator; William Allen, Owen's Quaker partner, immensely admired his schools, and it is not always remembered that Charterhouse in 1818 adopted the monitorial system, only to discontinue it after a melancholy falling-away of the eager new entrants. The vaticinations of Mr. Giddy, M.P., in destroying Whitbread's Bill of 1807 for the instruction of Poor Law children, were more representative, and possibly more prophetically accurate:

The scheme . . . would be found to be prejudicial to the morals and happiness of the labouring classes; it would teach them to despise their lot in life, instead of making them good servants in agriculture and other laborious employments to which their rank in society had destined them . . . it would enable them to read seditious pamphlets, vicious books and publications against Christianity; it would render them insolent to their superiors.

The Committee of the Privy Council on Education was established in 1839, by royal action, *since there was no other way of overcoming the obstruction in the Great Reformed Parliament*. Even as it was, a resolution deploring it went happily through the Lords, and failed by two votes only in the Commons. On top of this scarcely impressive demonstration of zeal for education came the battle of the religious, which seems, so far as dates can be a guide, to have been touched off by the worthy Mrs. Trimmer's intemperate championing, in 1805, of Dr. Andrew Bell against Mr. Joseph Lancaster. However that may be, by the middle of the century the sectaries were in full cry, and as Forster mournfully remarked, 'The religious difficulty is a most formidable difficulty in Parliament, but a very small one as between the parent of the child and the schoolmaster, and still smaller between the schoolmaster and the child'. In fact, as concerned those who were really caring for the children, there was no difficulty at all; 'Suffer the little children' was adequate

[1] The original phrasing; more illuminating than the normal misquotation.

enough guidance; what happened in the mid-century, as still happens to-day, fortunately to a rather less extent, was a naked and obscene struggle for power between the pundits of the several sects, who preferred to see the children decay in ignorance rather than have them enlightened by members of another communion. '*Tantum religio . . .*' this struggle delayed the fulfilment of even the Newcastle Commission's miserable charge, 'to consider and report what Measures, if any, are required for the Extension of sound and cheap elementary instruction to all classes of the People', until 1870; and still bedevils the public relations of L.E.As. and the Ministry. Public school enthusiasts, themselves a product of the sweet concordat whereby the Dissenting manufacturing classes, over-awed by the tremendous Christianity of Arnold and his fellows, meekly accepted the *imperium* of the clerical headmaster as the price of a sound moral training with some increased physical amenities and good social openings for their sons, are apt to forget or to overlook the sterile bitterness of the sectarian controversy; they should refurbish their history and observe how many of the black-listed schools of to-day are the direct result of the passionate desire of the orthodox to put up any and every kind of building which would serve to save their parishioners' infants from the better, but Godless, School Board erections. But, as if these handicaps were not enough, mid-Victorian retrenchment then took a hand. Lancaster's penny-a-week vision had not proved true in practice; school-building grants were rising; Kay-Shuttleworth was paying out money for pupil-teacher training and all manner of new-fangled if minute purposes: God knew what it all might amount to, and 9*d*. or 10*d*. still on the income tax. Accordingly, Robert Lowe, who should be burnt in effigy on every anniversary of the passing of the 1944 Act,[1] in 1862, with the unforgettable words 'if it is not efficient it shall be cheap', fastened for over thirty years the horrors of the Revised Code on English (not Scottish) elementary education, put learning by rote at a premium,

[1] And only granted a year's remission of purgatory for his attack on the stringent Latin-grammar type of curriculum.

destroyed all incentive to teach above the bare minimum required for the Payment-by-Results examination, reduced effectively the employment of qualified teachers (and even of pupil teachers) in the schools, and turned the inspectors from the friendly critics Kay-Shuttleworth and Matthew Arnold had hoped they would be into inquisitors whom it was the teacher's chief concern to outwit in every possible way.

Payment-by-Results and the Revised Code have been dead nearly sixty years, since when, with the consequent setting free of the state teachers—though the types remain—the curriculum and conduct of the schools of the state has changed out of all recognition. Lowndes' *Silent Social Revolution* exaggerates the difference very little, if at all; the almost complete disappearance of truancy as a major problem attests it no less. (Present-day truants, save for the collectors of railway-engine numbers, are almost all 'maladjusted', or products of unhappy homes.) But the past history needs recalling, if only because so many of the protagonists of the private sector seem to be living mentally in the days of the Revised Code. Thring, that great headmaster, founded the Headmasters' Conference at a date when the dreadfully nagging provisions of the Revised Code were at their height; it is not surprising that his loudest word was *No*, and that his Headmasters' Conference, as R. L. Archer put it, was brought up to be an educational House of Lords, refusing consent to every innovation. The alleged response of the head of a Direct Grant school to a suggestion that he should apply to his L.E.A., 'I would rather be eaten by lions than Gnawed by Rats', is justifiable on the supposition that he believed the Revised Code to be still in operation—as public education is not a public school subject, he may well have been unapprised of its abolition.

Nevertheless, the fact that administrative machinery was the essence of the state system, and that education, in the real sense, only got in as a result of the professional and economically disinterested enthusiasms of the practitioners, accounts for quite a lot, in particular for the technico-professional character of the conferences of persons engaged in the public sector. Anyone from outside, attending one of these gatherings for the first time, is apt to rub his eyes and wonder, amid all the earnest argument about 'Circular 0041', 'T Branch', 'Form 169 BC', 'Ministry Memorandum 326', 'My Authority's Practice', etc., what has become of education and its victims or beneficiaries—whether he has not got by mistake into the Annual General Meeting of the Institute of Sanitary Engineers or a conference on sewage disposal. And though, as anyone who has worked in public education knows very well, such a snapshot impression would be highly misleading, since a concern to devise the right formula for extracting money from the Treasury or the Comptroller is not at all incompatible with a passionate and individual interest in those for whose benefit the money is to be spent—the previous pages will have made it clear why so much of that interest is directed to the removal of stepped classrooms and trough closets, the provision of proper headlighting and suchlike material necessities—nevertheless, the impression of public education as something mechanical, niggling and unpurposed does remain. Nor is the disadvantage counterbalanced by the faults on the other side, when the public-school man, fresh from observing what can be done in a school of a few hundred hand-picked children—the 'hand-picking' being equally the case whether the school is traditional or ultra-modern—with large funds and a staffing ratio of 1 : 12, or, if he be historically-minded, having studied the achievements of Owen at New Lanark or the Hill brothers at Hazelwood, demands in a tone less of enthusiasm than of patent pained superiority why obviously sensible solutions are not instantly put into practice for some millions of children and hundreds of thousands of teachers. No doubt, this critic has much right on his side; we have known, to a great extent and for a very long while, what ought to be done about education. Owen told us how to run an infant school 140 years ago; Matthew Arnold's evidence to the Taunton Commission gave a picture of a coherent educational system which the 1944 Act has not yet achieved; Michael Sadler in 1908 drew a firm design for post-school education estimated then to cost in rates and taxes combined the sum of £1,000,000 per annum;[1] as recently as 1942 the Trades Union Congress produced a plan for further education-cum-apprenticeship of which, even in the excited and hopeful discussions of the war years, little notice seems to have been taken. We know much of what we ought to do; but for generations we just do not do it. Hence the weary irritation with which the practical educator receives the diatribes of the privateer; hence, too, the element of frustrated Utopianism and/or nobly-enunciated platitudes apparent in so many conferences on New Steps in Education. Somehow a real socialist programme must marry the two forces.

One other historical fact about English public education must be recorded. As I have said, it is apt to give an impression of lack of purpose. The reason is simple: historically it had none save the purpose of the sanitary engineer. In countries which underwent physical revolution, whether of a political or of a religious kind, in France, Prussia, Scotland, Japan, Nazi Germany, the U.S.S.R., it was imperative to teach the new values positively to the children, lest the work of the revolution be undone. Even in the U.S.A., children could not be trusted to find the 'truths self-evident' of the Declaration; they had to be taught to the native-born and still more to the immigrants from the Old Immoral World. (Whatever critics may think of the final result, American schools have undoubtedly and consciously taught 'American values'.) But the England of Lowe and Newcastle had no new values which it wished to teach to the children of parents who could not afford 9d. a week; consequently, all that was taught to them were the ancient values of Christianity, or so much of them as survived when Church and Chapel had done with their apostolic blows and knocks, nor was there any prescription of culture or of curriculum beyond the bones of the three R's and some needlework. One fortunate, but wholly undeserved by-product of this economy-utility policy was that nobody cared how the Grant was earned so long as it was earned. Teachers could try

---

[1] The 1952 estimate of the L.C.C. alone for further education was over £3½ million exclusive of capital.

any method they felt capable of trying, with the result that as soon as the strait-jacket of the Code was removed they were free to experiment up to the hilt both with subjects and with methods—a freedom which alarmed even that very free-thinking Chief Inspector Edmond Holmes,[1] and caused him to meditate upon chaos in his retirement; they were not constricted by the fearful rigidities of courses and time-tables which are to be found in the public schools of Sweden no less than in those of the U.S.S.R. The amount of experimentalism which the last fifty years has seen in English public education—attested to by many inspectors' reports and now at last being popularised by the Ministry—would be unbelievable to those whose idea of 'experimentation' is bounded by Dartington and Summerhill; it is not primary schools, but grammar and minor public schools which have been clamped into the Procrustean bed of School Certificate and its like. Cramping by financial rate-regulation and form-filling, by rule as to the days of school opening, the amount to be spent on clubs and school journeys, the collection of milk-money and so forth, may be irritating, but is, I submit, less damaging to the soul of a school than central and meticulous prescription of time-tables and text-books; nevertheless, freedom is not everything, and it is surely desirable that schools and those who teach and are taught in them should have some clear idea what they are there for.

This consideration also holds good, though in rather a different way, for schools outside and partly outside the state system. They could not, of course, be accused of lack of purpose during the latter half of the nineteenth century; they had their own systems of governing and middle-class values which they taught consciously and vigorously, and the great headmasters, from Thomas Arnold to Almond of Loretto with his shorts and flannels, eventually adapted their curricula to fit their pupils for the vocational courses of Lit. Hum. and the like, which in turn fitted them for the life of ministers and imperial adminis-trators. (If Robert Owen had not, at the age of forty, turned from a practical educator into a soaring evangelist, the

[1] *What Is and What Might Be*, by Edmond Holmes (1911).

philosophy of the *New View of Society* might have developed into a comparable ethos for the community of the labouring classes; we shall never know.) But it is surely apparent that this system of values, and the faith inspired by it, is disintegrating before our eyes with the conditions to which it was appropriate. Henry Newbolt's stanza for Clifton Chapel—

> '*Qui procul hinc*,' the legend's writ,—
> The frontier-grave is far away—
> '*Qui ante diem periit:*
> *Sed miles, sed pro patria.*'

reads now like something from a distant age; and Dr. James's plea for segregated education for selected 'brilliant' children sounds a very different note from Arnold's sermons to Christian gentlemen. Faced with the rapid disappearance of the dependent Empire and of 'British prestige in the Middle East', and with the even more disconcerting disappearance of the good supply of domestic servants and of labour waiting eagerly to be called in to clear the drains, repair the switch, and do a host of other necessary and irritating chores, the English upper class is less and less sure of purpose, of what it wants to do or to tell anyone else to do; on the other hand, the lower classes, freed from unemployment and the depths of poverty, and in enjoyment of the Welfare State, possessed of a great deal more knowledge and general skill, and civic training, than the bulk of them used to have, are yet finding that this does not necessarily bring either peace-in-our-time or emotional security, and are tending to worry no less than their 'betters' about what they can or ought to do. Britain is, in fact, going through a change in her national position and outlook no less than that which Denmark experienced 100 years ago. The Danes, wise in their generation and with a situation undoubtedly much easier to cope with than our own, revised their system of education to meet it. We may not believe that a change in education can of itself change the values of a community; but we can at least get to work to see what we want and why.

There is good reason to speed up with our thinking. For, as

I have already pointed out, educational change has in the past come very slowly, and there are two reasons, one material and one immaterial, why we still cannot expect it to come fast. The material reason is simply the enormous number of children. They *will* be born; they *will* grow up—and fewer and fewer of them can be relied upon to die of poverty and neglect; they require more and more teachers whose training must be progressively improved; and they have to be taught in schools and colleges which are exceedingly expensive to build, rearmament or none. Even the high education budgets of to-day leave black-listed schools in full use, county colleges a dream in the air, and technical education half-starved.

Everyone knows these material obstacles to progress; not everyone, however, is quite so conscious of the immaterial blockage, which is the extreme conservatism of the English voter, of whatever party, towards the untried in education. This does not apply, for example, in the case of housing. Almost everyone now badly housed, for whatever reason, will jump at the offer of any kind of a new house, even though it is not at all his ideal of what a house should be. But he does not feel the same about a school; even if he has welcomed with apparent delight paper plans for a new kind of school, when it comes to making his personal choice he is extremely likely to cling to the evil which he knows, even if he knows it to be evil, rather than embrace anything unusual. This means that changes in education depend not only upon the supply of steel and concrete and of teachers, but also on changing the outlook of the adult consumer; and this may easily take more than a generation. But that does not imply that we should not start; if we do not start we shall never arrive. And it *may* take less long than we think; or piecemeal change, such as that described in the Ministry of Education's 1950 Report, may again produce a much bigger result than anyone could foresee at the time. The main may come flooding in.

What then are the essential purposes for a democratic socialist education in the modern world? I list them here as they occur to me, not setting them out in any order of importance:

1. It must be equalitarian, not in the sense of uniformity, but in the sense of 'parity of esteem' for every child in the country, whether that child is physically inside a school or not; it must rid itself finally of the idea that 'stupid' or non-bookish children grow into adults some years earlier than others.

2. It must be socially equalising, in that it must not aim at producing any separated class or caste.

3. It must be viewed as a continuous whole from infancy to maturity, and it must be available at any time in adult life.

4. It must provide, as a *universal* measure, the basic minimum knowledge and skills necessary for living in a modern industrial community. What these are should be thought out; they should not be needlessly multiplied by people who want to put everything in. Some of the purposes of education mentioned in later paragraphs will be achieved only by a part of those undergoing the process; but we should declare clearly that an educational system which leaves any single person, other than the completely ineducable, without (e.g.) the ability to read and use his own language, to calculate sufficiently for his own immediate purposes, to keep his person clean and healthy, to cope with his basic living requirements, and to understand the basic social rules of his own society, is a failure by the most elementary standards.

5. It must provide, for all its recipients according to their individual tastes and abilities, first-line training in the use of tools and equipment, both manual and intellectual, and the opportunity to pursue that training further. 'Tools', in this sense, may be typewriters or sewing machines or hammers or balances, telephone directories or libraries or comptometers—or human 'experts'; the essential point is that, as the sheer amount of knowledge in the world increases and the number of skills multiplies, it becomes increasingly impossible and wasteful even to try to teach thoroughly within the limits of school life more than a fraction of the things which any intelligent person would like to know something about or to try and do for himself. What is important is that the boys and girls—*all* boys and girls, be it reiterated—should be shown that the subjects are there,

and be put in the way of learning more about them with the minimum waste of time.

6. It should aim at producing a whole person, counteracting, so far as an education system can do so, the tendency towards specialisation and fragmentation of life and personality. This aim undoubtedly involves, to some extent, working against the grain of city development; nevertheless, the half-conviction of a great many persons, and not by any means only of psychiatrists and social workers, is that it must be done, otherwise a society which has overstressed economic and political change will be in danger of being wrecked upon its ignorance and ignoring of individual and social values. To this end, therefore, education must offer to every child

(*a*) the opportunity of artistic and creative work of his own;

(*b*) the opportunity of seeing and hearing as much good performance of as many kinds as possible;

(*c*) the opportunity of organising and participating in all sorts of outside-lesson activities—sports, camping, play-acting, photographic and animal clubs.

To try and summarise the possibilities in a paragraph would merely produce officialese; the point is to stress equally 'my own painting—collection—hobby', '*our* team's triumphs', and '*my* or *our* chance to see what we like doing done as it really should be done'. No one of these is more important than the others.

I should add that the importance of this purpose of education seems to have been much better grasped, on the whole, by the state schools than by the older foundations. The name of Marion Richardson, to take only one example, should be honoured by every educationalist in the country; but there are still too many whose minds hark back to the days of *Piano as an extra* and cannot grasp that these erstwhile 'frills' do really educate for modern life.

7. It should, of course, provide for high-level training for those of high quality in all 'university standard' or 'national certificate standard' subjects, technological, literary, scientific

or administrative. This necessity is universally accepted, and perhaps needs no more than the bald statement; later we may have to consider what provision would be adequate, how it could be made available to late or handicapped starters, and how adult non-university education can give the less obviously gifted, at any time during their lives, opportunity to improve and to enjoy such gifts as they have.

8. It must further, however, train a body of people capable of doing and ready to do the work which any given society needs to get done; its curriculum beyond the minimum, therefore, must bear some general relation to the likely distribution of jobs within the society. This does not mean that we should or could return to the idea of educating to 'live within one's proper station', or try to solve the coal problem by producing a new race of Bevin boys; but the satisfying of individual choice and capacity is not the sole aim of education. The social aspect— what society needs from its members—also claims consideration. It is of course up to society and to industry to make the jobs which it requires such as persons well-taught in school can reasonably be asked to undertake.

9. Following upon this, education must also aim at developing social as well as individual personality, by training its recipients in the techniques of social living; it must make for self-government, for the capacity to think—and to ask the right questions—before acting, for initiative and for the growth of leadership, and for the sense of responsibility and sense of public service, which, however difficult they may be to define or consciously to 'inculcate', are the essentials of democratic society. This is the newest and the most difficult job for the educational community as a whole; it is also of prime importance. For whether the managerial-technical society which we are now creating turns in this country into a Burnham or Orwell nightmare, a *Servile State*, or a socialist democracy, depends in very large measure on how far education can create social consciousness, ability and knowledge to take large views, and a concurrent ability to deal seriously and sympathetically with the myriads of tiny human problems which arise in any large

organised society. Thirteen years ago I wrote that a modern society must have a double vision; 'it must think of, and regard as equally important, two types of problem—to arrange for the production and transport to millions of breakfast-tables of millions of eggs in shell, and to provide for the care and training of six delinquent children in Bermondsey'. I would say the same to-day, and would add that this double vision must first be learned in school.

10. Finally, an educational system must do its best to educate the handicapped of all types. At long last, this also is generally accepted in principle, though the delay and the high cost of 'special' education slows down its implementation. It may be observed, however, that just as ordinary health services learned much from the study of disease, so the experimental work upon educational casualties is teaching us a good deal that is of value in the education of normal creatures. The cost is not all net cost.

In a single chapter of a book, it would be impossible and foolish to try to lay down how these listed purposes could be carried out in day-to-day working; in any case, curriculum and technique of teaching are primarily the business of the teacher, and it would be an impertinence on my part to try to tell teachers how to bring on potential leaders, how to introduce children to Shakespeare and the musical glasses, how much time (and for which children) to allocate to 'project work' or visits to ballet or museum. If I knew how to do this, I should be a teacher, or at least an inspector running around from school to school offering suggestions and criticisms. (It is not always realised how much of the spread of educational experiment should go to the credit of the inspectorate, national and local.) I am very glad that recent developments in training colleges show a great desire to think out and try out new types of technique. Schools, however, and other educational institutions are highly individual entities; what will suit one will not suit another, and continuous experiment, with continuous comparison of results, is what we need. Three things, however, may perhaps be said.

First, that whereas a complete code by law established, prescribing what every schoolchild in Division X must be studying at 9 a.m. on the second Monday of the autumn term, is both un-English and a horrible idea, complete anarchy is not the necessary alternative; and it may be that we have gone too far in making no prescription at all. Here is a point meriting further discussion.

Secondly, that the Revised Code examination, the Special Place examination, and the late School Certificate are not the only, though the largest, offenders against educational values. Some university degree courses—more of the qualifying courses for entry to various professions—are so illiberal, so time-wasting, and so thoroughly *stupid* as to make angels weep. If we want to keep our managers and professionals whole men and not lopsided machines, it will be necessary to take some of the august gentlemen who control examinations, knock their heads together, and invite them to contemplate the bodies of their victims.

Thirdly, that we must not expect an educational system, here or elsewhere, to do more than is reasonable, or to advance much beyond its surrounding mental terrain. A school, or a whole set of schools, with live Heads can do quite a number of things in a limited field—build kilns, play a new sort of game, work continuously in the open air. But when it comes to social values, the schools in any one area cannot jump violently ahead of the neighbourhood or teach effectively values greatly at variance with those of the community as a whole. Even a single school, if it tries to do so, runs a great risk of turning out pupils who will commit suicide when they find out what the world is really like. A single school may find the risk worth taking; an L.E.A. cannot.

If the questions of technique and curriculum have to be left largely in the hands of those who will have to do the work, what is to be said about the shape of the educational system as a whole, the framework in which the teaching is to be done? This is not a subject which can be left undiscussed, particularly as it includes the only really burning question of the day—the future of 'segregated' education.

I shall begin by assuming the general acceptance of the Hadow reorganisation, though I am aware that there are still some who question it. I am, however, myself well-convinced, on experience, that there is an age somewhere between ten and twelve at which a child ceases to be a *little* boy or girl and is ready to begin a secondary (though not a specialised secondary) school education; and that, therefore, the existing private prep-schools which retain boys to the age of thirteen are making an educational as well as a social mistake.

One would begin, then, with the nursery school, not compulsory, I should hope, for a very long time, but highly desirable in an industrialised society of small families. One would then proceed to the primary school, where, again, there is little to be said, except to press on with improvements to the state foundations. If the standards of nursery schools could be made universal in primary schools there would be little need for anyone to bother about private ventures; it is fairly safe to say that no parent, except in a very few cases, would want to pay for primary education if the state school were such that he really felt the child was being well looked after. Unfortunately, people do not send their small children to school 'with the state'; they have to send them to the particular school which is at hand, and if that school is a disgrace to a democratic community, as it still is in more instances than I care to contemplate, there is nothing to be done but to agitate for its improvement. Improvement, however, with the consequent 'freezing-out' of a number of dressed-up dame-schools, is a matter of allocation of priorities—nothing more.

But when we reach the secondary stage, we run straight into the major problem. I must begin by stating unequivocally that I do not believe that any socialist can call any educational system socialist or even democratic which does not bring children together in a common school life, whatever their parents' income or previous history. If there is any other system in operation, it may have any merit you care to ascribe to it, but it is not socialist; and I have already given reasons for believing that a not very staggering increase in expenditure would make a common primary school system a practical reality. Beyond that, however, we enter the realm of vested interests and emotional attachments, of the Old School Tie, of the fear of 'Americanisation', of the bogy of size, of the rival propaganda of boarding-schools and of co-educationalists, and finally of the demand for the segregated education of an elite. Let us try to get the lines of argument at least sorted out.

I believe that the democratic socialist argument for common school life is as strong in secondary as it is in primary education. I do not see how any socialist can find it a good thing that children of different social classes should be separately educated or that, supposing present class distinctions to be obsolescent, children of outstanding intellectual gifts should be skimmed off the ruck and trained to be leaders, professors, managers, or what you will. To place your potential leaders at secondary school age in a forcing-house away from contact with their less gifted contemporaries, to whatever extent you may claim to be able to cultivate special skills in them, seems to me to destroy their own right to that wholeness in education which we have earlier postulated, to lower the level of school life for those not so selected, to be a flat denial of principle, and further to be a very dangerous means of promoting the totalitarian managerial type of society which we all allege we fear. Nor do I feel that parents of means should be able to purchase superior types of education for their own children which the latter have failed to achieve by other methods of selection. I am aware, of course, that this attitude presupposes the existence of highly sensitised means of selection, in which we could do much better than we do at present. I admit, also, that the rights of religious minorities have to be preserved by any practical statesman, though practical statesmen may well feel that sufficient concessions have already been made to the stronger sects. I would further add that it might be wise to promote experimentalism in the wilder sense by allowing parents to contribute to the cost of their children's education in very odd schools, since this is hardly likely to lead to any new class-alignment. The greater variety, the healthier the system.

The question of segregation or non-segregation is ultimately a question of principle, on which compromise is not possible. But we are very far from the ultimate stage, and it is certain that compromise, in the sense of several co-existing systems, will remain for a considerable time to come. Not even the most die-hard supporter of common schools has proposed the instant suppression of the grammar and public schools of the country, particularly in face of the 'bulge' which is due to enter in three or four years' time. It is therefore permissible to ask why the opponents of 'comprehensive high schools', which is not a new device first thought of in 1951, have suddenly allowed themselves to get so hot under the collar.

'Comprehensive' schools are only one of several possible means of achieving common secondary education; other suggestions are 'multilateral' schools built around a common campus, or a simple combination of two or three schools under a common board of governors for common out-of-school activities. The school plans of L.E.As. include specimens of all these as well as of bilateral schools uniting grammar and technical, or technical and modern, and plans which say in effect 'no change from the present system'; it is, however, the comprehensive school around which the ideological argument is raging.

A comprehensive school is planned to enrol all the children of secondary school age within its area, and gradually to sort and resort them into educational groupings according to their various abilities and interests, there being also many other groupings—athletic, dramatic, as well as the social groupings commonly referred to as 'houses'—which would not necessarily coincide in any way with the others. The *a priori* logical reasons favouring the comprehensive school are perfectly clear. There is the democratic argument; the techniques of living-together can be fully and satisfactorily developed only by people who do actually live together; anything else is a *pis aller*. Secondly, it is not disputed that if a wrong judgment is made about a child's capacity when he is eleven years old, this can be put right with far less heart-burning and far less social shame if he can be transferred to a different course within the same institution than if he has to be thrown out into a school which all his neighbours believe to be inferior. No device can be found which will prevent some humiliation to a child who turns out to be less of a budding Einstein than he appeared at ten years old; but at least social disgrace need not be added to intellectual disappointment, and I have yet to see any other solution which even purports to achieve this end.

Thirdly, the growth of school loyalty and sense of community is very much more easily achieved if the school really is one school and not a collection of yoked entities. Fourthly, a school which could afford a large staff and variegated equipment would be able to maintain teachers of high qualifications in various specialities, so that a child who, admitted as a 'grammar school type', found as he grew up that his interest was turning to the technical world would be able to find on the premises teachers who could show him, before his mind was finally made up, what a really good engineering course was like. Fifthly, and arising therefrom, a comprehensive school need not be tied to the tripartite division between grammar, technical, and modern, which, for all its adoption by important government committees, is really highly artificial (it does not appear in the 1944 Act): it could develop new types of combined courses, new 'Triposes', as it were, for the schools, which would really aim at suiting the education to the child—a thing now difficult to assure even for the brightest. (If anyone believes that such a development would result in the 'Americanisation', *in sensu obsceno*, of the school programmes, he is paying a very poor compliment to English tradition and to English teachers.) Logic and ideological arguments are not, however, enough: comprehensive schools are a new idea, and besides the stout defenders of privilege and those who are emotionally attached to individual schools (sometimes very inferior schools!) and fear their extinction, there are undoubtedly many who are simply apprehensive about this new thing, and do not want to try it even once. There is one strong argument used on their side, as well as some very silly ones, including the suggestion that comprehensive state schools are bound to produce a ferociously-imposed uniformity—if such a uniformity exists anywhere to-day, it is not in the county secondary schools but in certain public schools which had better in this chapter be nameless, but are well enough known to the unfortunate junior masters who have worked under their dictatorial heads and endeavoured to work on their oligarchic prefects. The strong argument, however, is the dislike of big schools, and that is so widespread that it cannot just be brushed aside.

I have already said that the assertion that a big English school *must* be just like a big American school is prejudiced nonsense; I would add that the notion that there is an ideal size of school which can be ascertained seems to me equally fantastic and to be flying in the face of all our past experience. Thring stoutly and successfully maintained that Uppingham should not increase beyond 320, because that was the largest number of boys of whom the Headmaster could have personal knowledge; this is a tenable position, but it rules out of court Eton, St. Paul's, Manchester Grammar School, and most of the major foundations. If once we allow that schools do increase their numbers beyond the range of the Headmaster's personal acquaintance, then I must confess I cannot see the overwhelming difference between a school of 600 and one of 1,500 or 2,500. (I am not accepting Dr. James's remarkable calculation that the really clever boy could not be adequately catered for in a comprehensive school with less than 5,000 pupils.) It depends, then, entirely, first upon the common sense and ability of the headmaster or headmistress, upon his power to delegate to deputies and to run his staff as a community, and secondly upon the arrangements made for smaller groupings and administrative and teaching units within the school itself. And that is a matter entirely within the competence of the authorities which are now proposing to set up comprehensive schools, and of the teachers whom they select. If what you want is a factory or a battleship, with the commander issuing his orders by loudspeaker laid on to every room, you can have it, though not, I am certain, without loud and probably effective protest from the staff; if you want a variegated community, made up of houses, teams, forms, sets, clubs, each with its own membership throwing up its own captains, chairmen, and secretaries, you can equally have that. The second course will certainly require more thought and pains, and it is to be hoped that the authorities intending to set up comprehensive schools are already taking thought and pains, and studying in detail both what has been suggested on paper and what has already been done experimentally in some areas.

On the question of numbers, however, the comprehensive school advocates are, in fact, prepared to agree that there is a real problem; they are not in love with mere size as such. Even that arch-scapegoat, the London County Council, facing the realities of schools laid flat or riddled with holes by war, sites at astronomical prices and the wartime generation knocking in new thousands at the gates—even its London School Plan is not tying itself to rigid numerical standards based on the tripartite estimate: its projected 'comprehensives' are of varying sizes. If that estimate could be forgotten, as in due course and with due experience it may be forgotten, it should prove possible to work a school of comprehensive type with a small but highly diversified top class on a considerably reduced enrolment. Meantime, it would seem to be a pity if the one bold suggestion of our time should be hamstrung and made into a bogy for good teachers because a short pamphlet from Transport House (which admittedly rushed its fences rather hastily) has given the word to all traditionalists to close into a herd and use their horns and hoofs upon the innovators, before English parents have been given a chance to see what an English comprehensive school is like in practice, and to compare it with what they have known before.

For there will be ample time and room for comparison. Apart from the slow pace of school-building, there are many authorities whose plans follow the traditional path; even in London the 1947 Plan, carried out completely, would leave a great number of grammar schools still untouched. Some of the correspondence in *The Times* and elsewhere would lead one to imagine that all the traditional foundations were going to disappear to-morrow or be turned into old trade unionists' homes or boarding schools for the educationally sub-normal: this is not the case. Particularly, it is not the case with the 'great' public schools; the lively speculations about their future made in many quarters in the 'thirties have proved quite inaccurate. Even if we could afford, during the next few years, to throw away usable secondary education, it is clear that their educational standards, their social prestige in a mixed society, and the matrix of emotion in which they are bedded will for a very long time, at least, preserve Eton, Harrow, and the other big foundations as Oxford and Cambridge have been preserved for much the same reasons, and that anyone who counts on their early disappearance is living in Cloud Cuckoo land.[1] But, as the recent storm of excited letters shows, they do themselves to some extent realise that the condition of survival in a modern age is to modernise; and if destruction is ruled out, reform is not.

There are five main directions in which reform could be sought. First, in the revival of the Fleming Report, which socialists, in the wartime flush of educational enthusiasm, treated far too cavalierly; entry to the public schools should be made at least as open as entry to Oxford and Cambridge. Secondly, these schools must be brought into much closer integration with the state system. This will, of course, involve some technical difficulties, since their 'catchment area' tends to be regional where it is not national; it probably implies in the end some regionalisation of state education which cannot be worked out here. But it could be done, once it were accepted, as I believe it would be by the more enlightened headmasters, that these schools cannot get out of their social obligations by sitting in proud and powerful isolation, but should make their contribution to the education of the whole country in an organic

[1] A more drastic redistribution of income and property might freeze out some of the lesser and less efficient kind. For that there is much to be said but it would be unwise to count even on that. They may be an anomaly and an offence to equalitarian sentiment; but so, strictly, is the Monarchy, which no one now proposes to abolish.

fashion, not merely by running a school mission or setting aside funds for boys' clubs in poor urban areas. Thirdly, the composition of their governing bodies should be looked into, even if this causes a fearful fuss,[1] otherwise opening the entry may easily become a farce. Fourthly, the autocracy of their headmasters should be diminished, and the position and status of assistants improved at least to the level enjoyed by those working in state schools. Fifthly, they should accept the Hadow age; those which, being boarding schools, may find it difficult to start their pupils so young, should nevertheless take responsibility for them, by some form of arrangement with the schools from which they come. With the day schools this problem need not arise, as it does not with the girls' high schools.

The last of these problems is only a problem because of the peculiar British boarding tradition. The line of Labour thought on boarding has been changing a good deal, mainly as a result of wartime experience, since the days when the word 'boarding school' was purely a class symbol; the advocates of home *versus* institution are now fighting their battle (which to some extent will always go on) more on grounds of educational theory and preference, and general opinion seems to be moving to the attitude that some experience of communal life is a good thing for nearly all children, not merely for those who must for one reason or another be taken from their homes. Ideally, this should mean that schools or groups of schools in town areas should have 'country complements', as it were, to which whole parts—years, or forms, or houses—would be transferred for periods long enough to make the experience a real one, continuing their school education meanwhile. Such a system is at present a good way off, and for London is very difficult indeed: but we should work towards it where we can.

The discussion in the foregoing paragraphs does not cover the whole field of education—far from it. I have written it at length because if we are to think sensibly about the future the most

---

[1] Even bodies like universities and colleges, when appointing governors to foundations in which they 'have an interest' are far too apt to choose a retired old gentleman or old lady living in the neighbourhood whose only concern with the school is to keep up its social tone.

important topics are the right understanding of past history, the present system, and the problem of a democratic secondary education. Other aspects, to which I now turn, though only a degree less important, are to that extent less controversial, and so can be dealt with more briefly. They all relate to those who have left school.

The crying need for better technical education at highest level is so much a matter of common agreement among everyone, whether they hold a brief for or against the Coca-Cola State, that I need do little more than underline it. This is another clear case where we have known for many years[1] what we ought to do, but have not done it; technical education has had a melancholy undernourished existence, varied only by occasional shots in the arm such as Whiskey Money, Messrs. Mather and Platt's continuation schools or the City and Guilds; the inferior social recognition of a night-school graduate in technology compared with a Redbrick university full-timer is still noticeable. Technical education needs now a fresh shot of considerable size, but, I would add, applied to existing ventures and not to the creation, with much paper, many committees, and no bricks, of a shadow of the Massachusetts Institute or Cal. Tech. To run off after this hare for reasons of prestige will, under prevailing circumstances, produce talk and nothing else. Let us build more on Imperial College at Kensington, the big Polytechnics, Manchester College of Technology and the other good provincial colleges.

And let these institutions take care of technical research, as well as of degree, diploma, and National Certificate students, whole-time and part-time, as they are doing now. Mention of part-time, however, takes me on to my second point, that of the normal school-leavers.

It is a fine bit of irony that to-day, thirty-four years after the Fisher Act, we should still be only talking about compulsory

[1] Ever since we were told by the Prince Consort, in fact. The reason for the delay is in part the influence of that strong personality Robert Morant, with his love for the classical curriculum in which he had been brought up; this does not make it any the less humiliating to receive well-deserved lectures on productivity from visiting Americans.

day continuation. In the controversy about sixteen *versus* county colleges, I am on the side of the county college; but the controversy is aerial, since at present we have neither, only some designated sites and a handful of voluntary day-release students. It is, I suggest, impossible for any socialist to accept that education, for any child, terminates when he is fifteen or even sixteen; and I therefore suggest, as the goal, that any child who goes to work before he is eighteen, should go to work *by permission of the Education Authority*, and not go to day or county college *by permission of the employer*. If that angle of approach were accepted, so that no child could enter employment of any kind save on the understanding that employment was part of the educational process, the precise proportion of time allocated to formal education, whether in county college, school of art or commerce, technical college, or whatever, would fall to be determined by the facilities presently available —nobody really believes that one day a week is enough. But it follows that any employment after the statutory leaving age should be regarded as apprenticeship, and that the 1942 proposals of the T.U.C. about apprenticeship to the industry, rather than to a particular employer—in which the building trades were then interested—should be further explored. The prior right of education being by these and other means secured, it may be that in the end we shall not need to worry too much about universal raising of the statutory leaving age: once employment of juveniles ceases to mean exploitation, it may be possible to admit that some types educate themselves better outside four walls—but not while street traders still bombard county councils with illiterate demands for the freeing of juvenile assistants from horrid restrictions on their working hours.

As to universities, the third item in our final agenda, the main immediate task of socialists is to hold the fort, to resist current agitation to reduce the war and post-war number of university students, whether the argument is based upon a supposititious over-production of graduates resulting in an unemployed clerisy which will be a seeding-ground for Fascism —an argument which, whatever its force in some countries, has no meaning at all in a country where graduates are so few and the demands of the teaching profession (to name only one) so high—or on a contention that there are not enough persons 'capable of profiting' by university education. The adherents of the latter cause brandish the figures of failures in final examinations as a proof that already too many of the people of Britain are being sent to college at the public expense, and generally conclude their speech or letter with an omnibus reference to the horrors of American universities, cheerfully equating Harvard with any hick-town academy. To evaluate the argument, however, we have to make up our minds what we want from universities.

Nobody suggests that we should lower the upper standard or make first-class honours mean less than they do, even if it may reasonably be suggested that examining bodies should be encouraged regularly to search their hearts and their syllabuses. Nor would anyone wish for a high percentage of failures in the lower ranges, since failures in general imply misfits. But since such tests as we can make seem to show that even now admission is a chancy business and that a good many of those who do not succeed in getting to a university are as 'fit' as those who do—it is nonsense to talk as though the ladder had now done all that was required of it, and that in future there would be no potential leaders remaining in the ranks—and since we have already assumed in the case of boarding schools that community life is a very valuable form of education, it seems not unreasonable to suggest that not merely should existing university education be stretched to its utmost, and expanded with rather less glacial slowness[1] than hitherto, but also that new second-line colleges should come into existence, to provide both for the misfits and for those who have at present no chance of getting in.[2]

These colleges would be local, of course, run for the most part by an L.E.A. or regional centre of education if such were in

[1] It was in 1898 that Sir Graham Balfour announced that very soon a university for North Staffordshire would be in being.

[2] There should, of course, also be an ever-growing provision of adult education of university and technical college standard available at any stage of life; this is particularly important in a country which pays lip-service to industrial democracy, but has no idea how to work it.

being; but they might also be established by a university as a kind of foster-child or by an educational trust, or in connection with training colleges. Teacher-training does not now deserve all the hard things that were said of it in the past, when training colleges took raw schoolchildren, herded them into something like a cross between an orphanage and a nunnery, crammed them for a year or two and then pushed them back to teach school until they were sixty-five—while others were lured into pledging themselves, at seventeen years old, to spend their lives as teachers, and having signed on topped up a mediocre arts degree with a year of pedagogics. The pledge has gone, and training college life is very different from what once it was; nevertheless, a good deal of the segregation remains, and segregation is not a good preparation for a career which is a human career calling for knowledge of all sorts and conditions of men, not a technique such as seamanship which must be acquired in a particular restricted environment. Combining a training college with a local college would do much to add to experience; in fact, if one looks far enough into a future of new and re-modelled towns, one begins to see something of an education precinct—a local college, a training college, a big high school, some park and playing fields, a swimming-bath, a restaurant and cafés, a theatre and other places where common post-school education and recreation can go on together.

For the final duty of an educational system is to take account of the lives and interests of the many who do not go, or have long since passed through, any college or similar institution, but who are men and women, citizens who need help to expand their own powers of enjoyment and creation and to overcome the frustration and loneliness which are the too-frequent results of the fragmentation of modern life. For all these groupings, brief or quasi-permanent, the educational system must be prepared to do what is required of it—to provide and clean and light the meeting-place, to supply the tools and materials for learning and enjoyment and the instructor or piano-player where one is needed. There is no controversy here, unless it be with a few extremists who have so fallen in love with the word 'community' that they want to force every natural solitary into a communal activity of some kind or other, or clamour for the building of 'community centres' in any and every location without enquiring whether there exists any community to use the centre. This rather comic over-enthusiasm, however, is not a serious matter; as a generalisation, nobody questions that we should do more of what we are doing.

This sketch of the future of education is incomplete. Incomplete, of course, in the sense that many questions which might have been discussed have been omitted; but incomplete also in that no sketch can show the millions of small decisions, of individual actions by persons of more or less authority, which can make all the difference, whatever the framework, between a good system and a bad one. (Anyone who has worked in public education must know the harm that can be done by a single act of apparent injustice or a single stupidly-phrased letter, and conversely how much confidence can be generated by vigilant humanism on the part of authority.) I have not been able to touch upon the importance of the voluntary factor, of the services of governors, managers, visitors, councillors, members of advisory committees and of parent-teacher groups —all the great unpaid whose story has yet to be written, but whose services may make all the difference between a totalitarian and a socialist state; that would be the material of another whole essay. I have not discussed how forces outside any formal system—the B.B.C. programmes, T.V., the press, etc.—influence education, though the election campaigns of 1950 and 1951, for example, made it clear that they do, and that education is only one part of the whole climate of social thought. Finally, it is incomplete, because I have assumed throughout without argument that we intend to work towards an egalitarian society. If we do, it is imperative that we try to shape our educational institutions so as to help and not hinder that purpose. If we do not, if the slight but perceptible recession since the hopes of 1944 represent a real trend, then we may as well stop planning altogether. We shall have had it.

THE ORGANISATION OF INDUSTRY
Austen Albu

IN 1951 the newly formed Socialist International, in its re-definition of the Aims and Tasks of Democratic Socialism, gave general recognition to the change in method by which, to quote Clause IV of the Labour Party Constitution, the workers by hand or brain were to secure 'the full fruits of their industry and the most equitable distribution thereof that may be possible.' In place of the 'common ownership of the means of production, distribution and exchange', the International recognised that socialist planning is compatible with the existence of private ownership in important fields, including those of small and middle-sized industries. 'Socialist planning does not mean that all economic decisions are placed in the hands of the government or central authorities. Economic power should be decentralised wherever this is compatible with the aims of planning.'

This declaration did no more than recognise the experience of those countries, and chiefly of Britain, which had taken into public ownership substantial sectors of their industry. However successful the nationalisation of basic industries has been in technical and economic terms, it has not satisfied the desire for a wider and more democratic distribution of authority nor built up any real measure of participation, by those engaged in them, in managerial decisions and their execution. This has been a disappointment to many socialists who never wished for a great concentration of state power, but who had none but the most hazy and Utopian ideas of any alternative. The lessons of totalitarianism abroad and the growth of the managerial revolution at home have underlined their anxiety; all the more so as full employment in a society which remains democratic is seen to create problems which need for their solution the widest possible popular sanction based on information and consultation. Consultation is the less successful the further it recedes from face-to-face discussion on the job; and the size and structure of industrial units and the degree to which they can exercise independent initiative are therefore seen as matters of supreme importance.

These arguments have led some socialists to accept the view that no further changes are needed in the way we organise our economic life other than to make existing public industry more responsive to popular opinion and private industry conform more closely to theoretical patterns of economic behaviour. But this is to accept a purely economic view of society which takes no account of the changes which have been taking place in industrial and social organisation, nor of the values which should underlie a socialist conception of society. To suggest that any large part of our economy can return to the highly competitive conditions of the middle nineteenth century or can emulate the supposedly ruthless struggle of American capitalism, is both to misunderstand the nature of modern technical and productive processes and, without any justification, to admit defeat for the socialist conception of a society whose predominant force is human co-operation.

Before new methods can be devised for the solution of these problems, it is necessary to ask how far the motives which have so far inspired socialists to advocate public ownership are still valid and what is the actual pattern of industrial society as it appears in Britain in the second half of the twentieth century.

The socialist attitude to the organisation and ownership of industry has passed through a series of changes which have corresponded to the rapid development of the Industrial Revolution and the capitalist system on which it was based. Socialists have always claimed that they were in the direct line of descent from those early leaders of revolt against the wealthy and the powerful, the peasant revolutionaries and the Levellers of the Civil War; and the same elemental urges towards social justice and equality which inspired them have continued to be the driving force behind socialist policies ever since. The Industrial Revolution, however, added a new and powerful factor of discontent when it broke up the traditional community structure and destroyed a system of class relationships which, although by the eighteenth century it had become cruelly insensitive to the great poverty which accompanied its wealth and culture, had remained with little change for hundreds of years and provided a relatively stable and secure existence in compact communities for the small population of the time.

The impact of the Industrial Revolution transformed the structure of society in an amazingly short time and the first movements of revolt by the new factory workers were directed as much against the changes in traditional social and economic patterns as against the unequal distribution of the rewards which the new system provided. It is not, therefore, surprising that the man who is generally considered the father of British socialism should have thought that what was needed was the development of a society in which the new techniques of production could be associated with the social and cultural life of small self-contained and self-governing communities.

As the process of turning the peasant and the craftsman into a member of the industrial proletariat proceeded, the emphasis of the attack on the capitalist system changed and became concentrated on the extremes of wealth and poverty which it created, and on the crude treatment of labour as a commodity in the processes of production and trade which it encouraged. *The Communist Manifesto* had provided an explanation in sociological terms of the violent social changes which were taking place and, in inflammatory language, described the effects of technical progress on the character of work as well as on social and economic conditions; on the other hand, *Das Kapital* was more concerned to explain in economic terms the causes of poverty and to concentrate the attention of socialists on the facts of capitalist exploitation. This suited the nature of the British working-class movement, based as it was, not primarily on a struggle for political objectives, but on the day-to-day demands of the growing trade unions for a larger share in the proceeds of the increasing wealth produced by the community; and, although it never accepted Marx's political ideas, it certainly swallowed what it understood of his economics.

The attack on exploitation was an attack on the profits that accrued to the owners of capital and was a sufficient motive by itself to inspire a vision of an alternative organisation of economic life in which all capital was socially owned. For many British socialists, however, an attitude at the same time more idealistic and more empirical provided the argument for the reorganisation of capitalist society. The early Fabians found in the use of private profit as the main incentive to industrial activity a motive both unworthy and inefficient; unworthy because it was subject to control by no code of ethical or professional conduct and inefficient because it was incapable of dealing in any reasonable order of priority with the urgent human and social needs of society. The predominant intellectual influence of the Fabians ensured that, while hatred of exploitation remained the driving force in the British Labour Movement, a tidy and schematic adaptation of existing political institutions became the framework within which its socialisation policy was to be worked out.

Serious opposition to Fabian ideas occurred only during two periods of disillusionment with Parliamentary political activity. The first lasted from 1908 to the collapse of the General Strike in 1926. This was the period of the growth of syndicalism in the trade union movement which took place after it was seen that the return of the first substantial body of Labour Party members to Parliament had not produced the results expected. From this insurrectionary wave was born the movement for industrial democracy which produced such elaborate plans for self-governing industries as those described in *The Miners' Next Step* and in the writings of the guild socialists. These were not without effect even on the Webbs themselves, who made some concessions to their ideas in their elaborate *Constitution for the Socialist Commonwealth of Great Britain*, published in 1920. But although they proposed a complicated structure which included a separate social parliament for dealing with economic affairs and a considerable apparatus of producer and consumer councils, these latter were never to be more than consultative bodies, and the management of socialised industry was to be in the hands of national boards which, while subject to direction on matters of major policy, should be solely responsible for day-to-day administration. The idea was no doubt taken from the constitution of the existing Port of London Authority, and it was used by Herbert Morrison in the only piece of socialist legisation introduced by the 1929 Labour Government, the London Transport Act. The benefits which he afterwards proclaimed should constitute a reason for nationalisation were primarily matters of efficiency and increased service to the public, although greater security and status for the workers in the industries were also mentioned. Unlike the Webbs, who proposed the inclusion of workers' representatives, he was opposed to any form of workers' representation on the Boards and, after the defeat of the Labour Government in 1931, this attitude led to a revival of the old controversy and an active movement for workers' control grew up. The T.U.C. supported the idea of the public corporation, but, led by the Transport and General Workers' Union, both the Labour Party and the T.U.C. finally agreed in 1935 that representatives of the unions in an industry should have a statutory right of representation on the board of management. In 1944, however, the T.U.C. report on post-war reconstruction no longer included a demand for direct representation, but used a form of words which has been virtually included in all the nationalisation measures. The view was expressed that the presence of direct workers' representatives might compromise the power of independent criticism and defence of the standards of the workers that were the main functions of the trade unions. It was suggested that among the qualifications that might be considered to render a person competent to be a member of the Board, experience gained in the collective organisation of labour should be included, and that a Minister might make his selection from candidates nominated by the T.U.C.

By this time, however, another factor had become dominant among the reasons with which socialists supported their arguments for nationalisation, the only form of social ownership to which the Labour Party gave consideration in its 1945 programme. The emphasis now was on planning for full employment and, although the written election programme supported the case for each nationalisation measure by arguments about co-ordination, greater efficiency and national service, the arguments used on the platform dealt far more with the necessity of controlling the investment of key industries, of curtailing the political and economic power of monopolies and of preventing the restriction of output which had been so prominent a feature of pre-war industrial policy. By 1950 the existence of monopoly remained the only criterion for outright nationalisation, but efficiency, restriction, shortage of particular products or the needs of particular regions remained as grounds for the establishment of socialised undertakings competing with existing private firms. The only other structural change proposed for industry was the extension of the number and possibly the powers of development councils; but without any suggestion that these should play any serious part in the policy or management of the industries they covered. The only reference to public ownership in the 1951 election manifesto was the promise to 'take over concerns which fail the nation and extend new enterprises wherever this will serve the national interest'.

The opponents of socialism claim that it is the failure of the nationalised industries that has made public ownership an unpopular policy and that for that reason the Labour Party has quietly dropped it from its programme. But the records show that most of these industries have been remarkably successful considering the conditions under which they were taken over, and, if the steam has gone out of Labour Party propaganda in their support, the reasons must be looked for elsewhere.

The objects which socialists have sought to achieve through public ownership, and which are still valid to-day, may be summed up as the prevention of exploitation through the excessive return to the owners of capital; the planning of the nation's resources for full employment; raising the efficiency of industry in the interests of the consumer and of our foreign trade; and the restoration of a feeling of participation and common purpose among the workers which is missing from capitalist industrial society.

The truth is that the most urgent of these objects of public ownership have now been achieved by other means. The dominating motive in 1945 of planning for full employment has been satisfied with only one-fifth of industry nationalised, and there is a growing view that, in so far as internal conditions are concerned, this can be continued. Nationalisation certainly prevents the increasing profits of an expanding industry going to the shareholders who, when they are compensated, become receivers of interest at rates determined by government policy. This remains an important feature of nationalisation because it prevents the continual growth in the wealth of the equity shareholder which is bound to take place in private industry under full employment conditions. But other methods have been found of redistributing the national income in favour of the poorer sections of the community and the increasing welfare of the working class has taken the edge off the feeling of exploitation. The taxation of company profits, limitation of dividends, price-fixing and the increased power of the trade unions have all contributed towards this end.

Whether or not the objective of increased efficiency, and therefore of greater service to the consumer, has been achieved is more arguable; certainly no better results would have been achieved if the industries had remained in the hands of their previous owners, and in the case of the airlines very substantial advances are being made. At a time of rising costs it is not surprising that the nationalised industries have been easy targets of criticism; what is disappointing is their failure to make people realise how much less their own prices have risen than those in most other industries and so to combat the more dishonest attacks made against them. If most of them have made no startling and obvious advances towards greater efficiency the reason will at least partly be found in their failure to create in their managers, technicians and workers any radical change of attitude towards their work and responsibilities. There has been among many socialists a mechanical and Utopian idea that the transfer of an industry from private to public hands would automatically result in its workers throwing off their traditional antagonisms and inhibitions and working whole-heartedly for the good of the cause. That this has not taken place is now generally blamed on the form of the public corporation or on the existence of so many in authority who held the same positions under the old regime. But this, of course, is much too simple an explanation. The problems of human relations which the nationalised industries face are due mainly to the size and complexity of their organisational structures and are faced equally by all organisations of similar size. It is, indeed, surprising that so little consideration was given in the past to the management structure that these industries would need below the top board level. In the *Reorganisation of the Electric Supply Industry*, published by the Labour Party in 1932, only one paragraph is devoted to this problem. Apart from the proposal to set up regional boards for distribution, the actual organisation of management was to be left to the national board.

No one to-day would choose, if it could be avoided, to set up under single control industrial undertakings as large as the National Coal Board, the British Electricity Authority or the British Transport Commission. But these were certainly special cases where the need for a rapid expansion of technical or managerial efficiency or the necessity for national planning of resources made a concentration of policy-making power at the centre essential. In fact, any attack on that concentration in these industries is an attack on the objectives of nationalisation themselves. From this point of view, the only question to be asked is whether it would not have been better to have established the control of policy firmly where it ultimately lies—in the hands of the Minister. Under the present circumstances the chairmen of the boards have become endowed with great power; they can use their positions to mobilise public opinion in the interests of their own industries sure in the knowledge that they will be defended in Parliament by the Minister to whom they are responsible. By making the Minister chairman of the board, it would be easier both to concentrate general policy-making and to decentralise day-to-day management. The form of the British Transport Commission, with its very small policy-making staff and its delegation of management to the separate executives set up on the basis of function, invites this change, which would also have the effect of increasing the public accountability of the boards through criticism and debate in Parliament. In the case of fuel and power, the present position of the Minister as the co-ordinator of policy is clearly too weak and will hardly be helped by the appointment of a super-co-ordinator, responsible also for transport, in the House of Lords. There is general agreement that managerial decisions should always be taken as near to the point of action as possible; but as long as it is necessary to retain the policy-making power at the centre the problem of the best method of decentralisation of management will inevitably vary according to the nature of the industry. To a large extent the problem is not one of the structure of the industry at all, but of the character and personalities of those engaged in it and of their relationships to each other. For decentralisation to be successful harmonious relationships must exist in an organisation and these can only be based on integrity at the top and confidence between its members at all levels. These conditions take time to establish and must be carefully fostered in a large organisation brought suddenly into being; on their growth the future of the industries already nationalised depends.

It is clear that in industries organised on such a scale the problem of associating the workers with their management is a very difficult one. It would be wrong to underestimate what has already been achieved, and as the boards themselves gain confidence and as managers and workers learn the habit of co-operation the machinery that has been established will grow in usefulness. What is finally required, as Dr. Elliott Jaques has pointed out in his book, *The Changing Culture of a Factory* (London, 1951), is a consultative system which will provide sanction for policy decisions and for an executive authority willingly accepted

K

by all the members of an industry. How to reconcile this conception of industrial democracy with the more primitive desire for self-government which activated the syndicalists, and which underlies so much current discussion on joint consultation, is a matter on which much research needs still to be done. It would seem, however, that there must exist some process by which all those employed in an industry are enabled to participate in policy decisions; either through directly elected representatives on the board or through a hierarchical system of joint consultation with considerable powers. In either case there must also be an increasing participation in the process of interpreting policy and of making decisions at subordinate levels.

The creation of a feeling of common purpose in the activities of industry still remains, therefore, one of the outstanding unattained objectives of socialist industrial policy. Without its achievement it will be extremely difficult to deal with the problem whose importance can now be seen to overshadow all other aspects of our economic life: how we are to balance our trading accounts with the rest of the world. With our population now over 50,000,000 people, with full employment and the abolition of poverty daily increasing our need for food and raw materials, with the growth of population and industrialisation in formerly backward countries creating a widening gap between manufacturing and agricultural production in the world, there can be no hope of the trend of the terms of trade turning again in our favour. Certainly we must seek new sources of supply and help their development by investment in under-developed countries abroad; but if we are to raise, or even to maintain, our standard of life we shall also have continuously to raise our production at home and increase the value of our exports.

If these things are not done the new society we have started to build with increasing democratisation of political, social and industrial life will be destroyed and a solution will be found which involves the return of the old compulsions of unemployment and authoritative power.

In view of our lack of indigenous raw materials, exports in the future will have to consist largely of goods involving in their costs of conversion from raw materials to finished products an increasing proportion, not so much of skilled workmanship, as of scientific research, technological development and managerial organisation. A great increase in technological education is overdue and is as important a capital investment as any other of the more obvious claimants. This in itself involves a revolution in the generally accepted scale of educational values and the destruction of the snobbish attitude that still exists in this country towards the processes of manufacture and those engaged in them.

One of the objects of the educational changes must be to find out the best brains in the community, to give them the fullest opportunities and to allow them to earn the highest rewards.

There need be no fear that this must mean a reversal in our progress towards a more just and equal society or any particular encouragement to competitive private enterprise; for the outstanding feature of modern science is its co-operative character and the scale of investment needed for its application. This has bred a type of scientific man who, whether he is engaged in pure research, in development of new processes or in the organisation of production, is accustomed to work as a member of a team within an organisation of which he and his colleagues are salaried servants. The increasing application of the social sciences to business management has narrowed the gap in outlook between the productive and the commercial branches in industry, and this, combined with the unit size of a large part of modern industry, is giving rise to a growing professionalism among their members. There can be little doubt that the incentives which move such men to work are not the crude self-interest of classical *entrepreneurs*, but a complex of half-conscious urges of which the spirit of the enterprise in which they work itself plays an important part. The habits, experiences and behaviour of these salaried officials of industry are in a different world from those of the small masters of true private enterprise and much nearer those of some branches of the Civil Service and of public industry to which they easily pass. Perhaps the main difference between them lies in the necessity, as industry grows in size and complexity, for the development of an *esprit de corps* based on a sort of bureaucratic morality among the members of the enterprise. This morality rests on an understanding of one's position in relation to those above, below and around one and generates a self-discipline which compels one to carry out one's duty without a continual external spur. In sociological terms this is an acceptance of function in a complex structure as the result of training and of the daily process of communication. In large enterprises successful communication between all its branches and individuals is the essence of morale and this itself is a technique which only the salaried servant learns. It takes place in many ways which include simple instructions or suggestions passed verbally from one level to the next; written orders or statements of policy; formal negotiations on wages and conditions and committees and conferences of officials or of managements and workers. One of the most used methods of communication is the filling in of forms, by means of which information can be collected from individuals, collated for purposes of control and disseminated to all who may be interested.

It is this different experience, and, if the process of job-selection has taken place at all in accordance with volition, difference of character and temperament that make it so difficult to fit the previous small private owner into the structure of a nationalised undertaking. What is readily acceptable to the former servant of a railway or large steel company is incomprehensible to the small road haulier whose workaday discipline collapses without the daily spur of profit and fear of bankruptcy. The truth is that, although there is a large penumbra in which they overlap, there are to-day two distinct types of industrial structure in which the true division is not to be found between what are conventionally called private and public industries, but between enterprises managed by their real owners and those which are managed by professional directors.

In what is traditionally called private industry this line of division lies roughly between the public joint stock company whose shares are freely transferable on the Stock Exchange and the private company or business partnership in which ownership and management conform to classical patterns. In the former, only the legal forms of control remain with the shareholders whose numbers and atomisation have for many years prevented them from exercising any initiative or real influence on the policies of their directors. These companies include all the large, well-established concerns which have long passed the period of risk of ordinary business failure. Before the war their main risk was that associated with the trade cycle, and, under conditions of full employment, their profits are bound to increase and their ordinary shareholders to receive in dividend and capital appreciation far more than the value of that risk to which their investment is still subject. Many of their directors recognise this themselves, and, even before the era of government-sponsored dividend limitation, preferred to increase their rate of dividend distribution slowly while using their profits to expand their businesses. Between the years 1928 and 1948, while the total paid-up capital of public companies increased by only 15%, the total capital which they employed, including their reserves, had increased by more than 50%. This was during a period which included the slump of the 'thirties and the years of the war; since the war, in spite of taxation, the rate of accumulation of capital by public companies, in money terms, has accelerated. Whether there has been an increase in terms of real assets is a matter of argument; but any such increase must lead to a growth in the power and independence of the boards of directors of these companies. It is in order to retain this power that they continually press for reduction in company taxation which would enable them to expand out of their retained profits, and so avoid having to seek fresh capital on the market. When they are not able to do this they frequently do not issue ordinary shares, but raise the new money in the form of loans or debentures at fixed rates of interest and carrying no voting rights.

It is clear that in many of its features—independence of its directors, professional management, growth of fixed-

133

interest capital—the public joint stock company is nearer to a public corporation than to the classical conception of private industry. The nationalisation of the steel industry made no change in the management structure of the enterprises of which it was composed, but substituted a single shareholder, the Iron and Steel Corporation, responsible through a minister to Parliament, for a mass of previous shareholders, few of whom could exercise any effective control. The only shareholders who had previously been in a position to exercise any influence over policy had been the institutional investors, including the insurance companies and the banks with their subsidiary finance corporations. The Corporation has now taken their place, but the Companies Act restricts shareholders to the function of electing the directors of companies, passing their annual accounts and agreeing on the disposal of the profits; and it is in this way that the Corporation would have to exert its influence.

What is needed is to make such changes in company law as will recognise the true nature of companies under present economic conditions and satisfy the socialist requirements of public responsibility and workers' participation. The scope of what is required can be measured by the fact that, although the number of public companies is only about 12,000, together with the nationalised industries they are certainly responsible for well over half the economic activity of the country; the remainder being in the hands of private companies, partnerships, individual employers including farmers and professional workers. Effective participation by public authorities in the policy-making of these companies would therefore provide a substantial measure of control over the whole economy and a far more satisfactory one than such external methods as licences or development councils. This could be achieved by the appointment by the government of a proportion of members to their boards of directors—such directors to be recruited by a special branch of the Board of Trade charged with the carrying out of industrial policy. This method would not upset the general structure or the corporate spirit of the best type of existing board in which the main body of members are full-time, active officials, many of them recruited from within the organisation. It is not suggested that such appointments would be necessary to the boards of all these companies; but the Board of Trade should be entitled by law to one share in every public company carrying with it, in addition to the usual right to receive reports and attend general meetings, the right of naming a number of part-time directors to the board if the Minister wished to do so. This right would be exercised in the case of companies whose activities had an important influence on employment, foreign trade, scientific development or capital investment. In 1949 over 40% of those employees engaged in manufacturing industry were working in establishments employing 500 or more persons, but the number of such establishments was only 2,382. Several of these establishments belonged jointly to a single company, so it is clear that, even when non-manufacturing companies are included, the number of companies which would be involved in order to ensure a sufficient degree of control is not excessively large.

The appointment of individuals as directors would not, however, be sufficient to ensure the influence of the government's views in the formulation of policy unless the Board of Trade were reorganised to cope with the planning duties that this would involve and if special steps were not taken to recruit and train the individuals concerned.

These proposals for introducing some measure of public responsibility into the activities of large companies would by themselves provide no answer to the problem of creating a feeling of common purpose and would do little to counteract the growth of the managerial revolution which has appeared to substitute a new authoritarian hierarchy for the old class structure. To these problems the old slogans of industrial democracy or workers' control by themselves offer no solution. Self-government in large and complex enterprises can never mean government without authority; the basis of participation in management must primarily consist in the sanctioning of policy and of executive authority. But the sanctions of the policy of an organisation derive not only from its own structure and powers, but also from the nature of its products and their market, from the national laws and regulations to which it must adhere and from the community standards which it must observe. These external forces undoubtedly limit the dangers of managerialism, but they would also prescribe the limits within which workers' participation in management could operate and they therefore provide an answer to those who foresee in such participation the growth of a syndicalist exploitation of the consumer. On the other hand, if policy within a company is to receive the sanction of those who work in it, then they must be represented in the place where it is formed: the board of directors. A further change in company law should, therefore, be made which would entitle those who work in any public company, if they decide to do so by ballot, to appoint a certain number of directors to the board. Once this had been done, the way would be open for an extension of the role of joint consultative machinery, not in order to provide for management by committee, but in order to ensure sanction for executive authority at all levels of the chain of management.

The introduction of the election of employee representatives to boards of directors or to the boards of public corporations would necessitate a reconsideration by the trade unions of their traditional outlook to individual companies. Heretofore any suggestion which involved the closer association by the workers of a particular company with its management has been frowned on as likely to weaken their loyalty to their trade union and so to endanger the general bargaining position of the union's members. But the task of representing the workers in an industry in negotiations over wages and working conditions has become not less, but more, important under full employment conditions and would continue to be so whatever the forms of management authority. Even the introduction of some system of national wage machinery would involve an elaborate process of professional representation of the claims of different groups for their fair share of the national income. The need for independent trade unions is as great to-day as ever, but a clear distinction needs to be drawn between these trade union functions and the functions of participation in management within a company or public corporation. Participation within every unit should arise from election by the whole body of workers concerned and, with the exception of the proposed directors, should be undertaken by those working in each establishment or department. These directors also should be elected, but the choice of candidate could well be widened in order to give the workers the opportunity to elect someone outside the enterprise who they felt would better represent their views. This would enable trade union officials to be elected, but the unions themselves would be well advised not to allow them to stand and so to confuse their two functions. The history of the Dock Labour Board is a warning of the dangers involved in doing so. The trade unions have established a right to consultation on national economic policy and it is here, and in the top levels of large industrial groupings, that their officials should make their contribution. In an individual enterprise the object should be to encourage the men and women who work in it to feel a direct, and not an indirect, responsibility for those who represent them in the making of management decisions. This is not to say that the unions would not have a big job of education and guidance to do for their members elected to these positions.

One further change is called for in the laws that govern public companies both by the logic of their present position and by the claims of economic justice. The dividends to ordinary shareholders should be permanently limited to an amount which might vary for different categories of company, but which should be no more than sufficient to cover the risks involved under modern conditions. The argument that is generally used against such a proposal—that it would stop the provision of risk capital—overlooks the fact that risk-taking in the traditional sense is hardly ever to-day the function of the public company. New companies are almost invariably private companies which do not raise their funds by public subscription, but from a few shareholders whose shares are not freely transferable on the Stock Exchange. The public companies rarely extend their activities in such a way as greatly to increase the overall risk to which their shareholders are exposed; as can be seen by the ease with which they can raise funds at comparatively low fixed rates of interest. Nor to-day do there still exist any substantial numbers of people willing and able to provide large quantities of finance for speculative enterprises with the possibility of a very high return. The function of financing industry is more and more becoming the province of institutions such as insurance companies, investment trusts and special finance corporations. These bodies are under the necessity of investing their funds as best they can, and there is no reason to think that they would be unwilling to continue to do so in industrial stocks merely because the maximum return they could get would be only a few per cent. above the gilt-edged rate. The introduction of permanent dividend limitation in these companies would have the effect of stopping the appreciation in the value of their shares and so of cutting off the most important remaining form of profit-making by increase in the value of capital. It would remove from the equity shareholder a hedge against rising prices which is not shared by those who put their savings into other forms of stock and to which he is not entitled by the function he now performs. Some part of the profits that would accumulate if dividends were limited should be distributed to those engaged in the enterprise, but the state should still be entitled to take in the form of profits tax or otherwise a proportion which might vary in accordance with the investment needs of the economy as a whole and of the industry concerned.

The changes here proposed in the legal form of the joint stock company are largely a recognition of the changes that have already taken place in its structure and motivation. Its directors and salaried officials, although undoubtedly spurred on by the thought of profit or loss in the annual accounts, are not themselves directly inspired by hope of personal gain. Their habit of daily co-operation, not only with their own colleagues, but also frequently with members of other firms and government departments, outweighs the crudely competitive instincts that operate in the breast of the small businessman. That is why it is both possible and necessary formally to associate in their control both the community at large and their own employees.

There would remain the large number of mostly small businesses run either by individuals or partners or, increasingly, by private companies with shares held by a family or small group of people. As a rule, in these businesses ownership and management are closely associated and the hope of profit and fear of bankruptcy are direct incentives to efficiency and enterprise. The title of 'private company', exempting the firm enjoying corporate status from the proposed provisions for public companies, should be restricted as far as possible to those enterprises in which these conditions apply. It is these companies that should form the mainstay of the true private enterprise sector of the economy, and steps should be taken to ensure that they do not take refuge in non-competitive practices unsuited to the way of life chosen by their owners. Subject to this proviso, however, there are good reasons for encouraging the founding of new companies of this type. While it is true that the large companies with their research and development staffs are to-day responsible for far more new products and new processes than originate in the brains of individuals working on their own, nevertheless the opportunity must still remain open to the single inventor to try out his idea at his own or his friends' risk. A stream of new entrants to the industrial field is necessary to keep existing businesses on their toes and to provide a range of companies of different sizes, even if only a very small number ever grow to be really big. No one yet knows the optimum size of unit for the purposes of management within each industry and, as the number of people capable of managing large organisations is limited, there is much to be said for allowing men of initiative to build up enterprises with which they grow themselves in experience and capability. In certain trades there are advantages, both technical and psychological, in small, self-contained working units where craftsmanship is predominant and supervision can be reduced to the minimum.

The financial facilities at present available to such companies are insufficient; for the existing finance houses are unwilling to assist a new and risky enterprise whose physical assets may be of little value and with whom the cost of investigating and negotiating the provision of a small amount of capital may well outweigh any possible return. Some new machinery is required to fill this gap, and further steps should be taken along the lines of the development area and new town industrial estates to provide factories and plant to rent. In order to assist these companies in the early days of their growth, there might also be some relaxation of taxation on their first profits ploughed back into their businesses. This might take the form of direct relief on profits actually used for expansion or of enlarged initial depreciation allowances on new plant, even to the extent of 100 per cent.

The effect of these proposals would be greatly to encourage the starting of new private companies and some of them would grow into large enterprises; but to judge from the figures of existing companies the number who did so would be very small. In 1949 the average paid-up capital of the 230,000 private companies then in existence was about £8,000 compared with a figure of £300,000 for the public companies, and there was no reason to believe that the ratio of average capital actually employed, including loans and retained profits, in the two types was very different. The incidence of death duties, however, compels the owners of a large private company to turn it into a public one by an issue of shares on or before the death of the founder. Contrary to the frequently expressed view, this can have no harmful economic result. On the first sale of the shares to the public a substantial block, sufficient to give control, is bound to remain in the hands of the heirs of the founder who, if they have been successfully employed in the direction of the business, will certainly be elected to the board of directors. If in succeeding generations the members of the family are unable to get themselves elected on their merits, there can be no argument for maintaining them in positions of authority in the company. In fact, British industry has suffered in the past, and still suffers to-day, from just this form of nepotism, and its disappearance can do nothing but good.

There is one form of enterprise well suited to small-scale manufacture, to which little attention has heretofore been paid: the producer's co-operative. The public provision of premises and capital on easy terms might be used to encourage associations of technical and manual workers to set up such societies for suitable types of manufacture. In view of the general growth of education that has taken place in this century, these might now stand a very much better chance of successful development than was possible in the past.

The proposals here made arise out of the application of socialist philosophy to an empirical study of existing economic institutions. The functions that a particular institution performs in a complex society are many and varied and not all of them are to be discovered in its overt aims and activities. It is the hall mark of Utopianism to make legislative changes and to break up existing institutions without due consideration of these functions and of the human relationships on which they depend. When the traditions of Christian duty and social responsibility which mitigated the ruthlessness of early capitalist society were destroyed by utilitarian rationalism, the continuing need for human relationships, other than those of the market, gave rise to the growth of voluntary associations. The Free Churches, trade unions and trade associations took the place of the traditional community relationships.

Gradually the increasing application of science has provided a new motive for co-operative association in place of the religious and social sanctions of pre-industrial society or the purely protective bodies that succeeded them. The truly individualistic, competitive man is once again seen to be unrepresentative of common humanity just as the era of genuine capitalist *laisser-faire* is seen as a short term deviation from the normal pattern of human behaviour. To-day the leaders of industry defend their institutions with talk of service to the community; and profit, in place of being an end in itself, has become an expedient. It is now time to take them at their word, to destroy the ambivalence of their position, and to bring the open, legal form of our economic institutions into line with the true functions which they perform. The purpose of this essay has been to try to show how this can be achieved without the disruption of existing working communities which are rational in form and which are not in themselves anti-social

TRADE UNIONS IN A FULL EMPLOYMENT ECONOMY

Ian Mikardo

THE structure of the British trade union movement was shaped by the environment in which it evolved. Its survival, like that of every other living organism, depends on its ability to adapt its structure to suit the quite different environment in which it now lives and in which it will have to live in the future. So far it has given little evidence of sufficient flexibility to accomplish that adaptation as quickly as is required.

Trade unions came into being as a weapon in the class war as it was fought in a *laisser-faire* economy. Because they were born into a world of industrial anarchy, they developed a fierce, *sauve-qui-peut*, jealously-guarded independence not only of all outside organisms but even of one another. Because they were created as instruments of struggle, they are not so readily usable as media for co-operation. Because they were trained to regard a government as merely an executive arm of the boss class, they lack the equipment for working with a government instead of against it. Because they were conditioned by a century of large-scale unemployment, their reflexes react slowly to the impulses of full employment. Because they created, and grew up with, only one working-class political party, they haven't developed a technique for dealing with a political division within their own class. And now they find themselves in a Labour-created, planned full-employment economy, distracted by Communists from within their midst as well as by the Tories from outside, and they are trying to breathe the air of this brave new world with the gills they developed for living in the flood of nineteenth-century capitalist anarchy.

Though they had had, from 1940 onwards, a foretaste of things to come, the trade unions were taken by surprise by the new conditions which followed the General Election of 1945. In those conditions, every strike was a blow not against an employer, but against their own Government and their own Party. Higher wages, which had formerly been the only means for giving the worker a bigger share of the wealth he created, were now represented as a threat to the success of budgetary action designed to achieve precisely that end. Increased productivity, which had formerly been the means of enriching employers and of putting fellow workers out of work, now became a means of helping their own Government and their own class. And the nationalised public corporation, their own brain-child, suddenly confronted them with the confusing spectacle of a boss who didn't belong to the boss class and a board which included a couple of their own members.

Even more fundamental than these obvious changes was one which went virtually unnoticed by the trade union movement because it had come about gradually. The growth of the joint stock company resulted in a divorce of ownership from management and faced the workers with a new class of professional managers who lived by the salaries they earned from their work and not from their ownership or part-ownership of the equity. In large and important sections of industry the self-reliant, dictatorial small-scale *entrepreneur* gave way to the hired manager or technician who was more interested in the successful exploitation of his managerial or technical skills than in the sometimes accidental fluctuations of the profit-and-loss account. Gradually the power of the hired manager increased and the power of the absentee shareholder—or at least the exercise of it—diminished. Slowly there began to evolve a new race of bosses in the factory who hadn't quite the same urge to take unfair advantage of workers as their predecessors had. Many of them began to study the art of labour relations, and even those who didn't condemn worker-exploitation because it was anti-social at least learned, in some cases, to condemn it because it was inefficient.

Few workers, and few of their leaders, understood—or wanted to understand—this change. They remembered the villainous exploitation of their fathers by past generations of employers, and they appreciated that some present employers were merely survivors from past generations. To differentiate between the new and the survivals from the old would have required an effort of thought. It was simpler to repeat mechanically that the leopard never changes its spots, and to ignore the fact that the leopard had retired to the hotels of Bournemouth and the hydros of Buxton, leaving an entirely different animal to run the factories of Treforest and the Great West Road. It was simpler to stick to national agreements and secure the minimum from the worst employer, rather than to deal with every case, or every group of cases, on its merits.

Here, then, was the strange new world which faced the trade unionist after 1945—a Labour Government, full employment, a planned economy, budgetary redistribution of national income between the *rentier* and the worker, nationalisation, and the interposition between him and his boss of a new race of professional managers.

The drastic reorientation of thought demanded by this metamorphosis was bound to be a long and slow process; but it would have been possible to take some emergency first-aid measures to deal with the new situation if there had been a single power in the trade union movement capable of making decisions and of securing their implementation. As it was, the decentralisation and diffusion of authority within the movement ensured that the class could learn only at the speed of the slowest or most obstinate pupil. Any one leader of any great union who was either unable or unwilling to understand the new situation could obstruct the progress of the rest. A Cripps might convince the General Council that new times demanded new methods, but the General Council had little power to induce, and no power to enforce, the acceptance of that conviction by the affiliated organisations.

The commonly-held concept of the T.U.C. as an all-powerful body capable of creating, and changing, the whole climate of industry is an illusion. The only executive powers exercised by the General Council are the power to raise levies and the power to adjudicate between unions in demarcation disputes. Any pronouncement which it makes on policy is not an enforceable ukase, but an exercise in peaceful persuasion. Even the resolutions carried by an Annual Congress, whether by acclamation or only by a mere majority of a few millions, have no binding force on the affiliated organisations. On more than one occasion a member of the General Council has put forward a statement on behalf of the G.C., secured its acceptance by Congress, and then found his own union pursuing a policy in conflict with it.

The difficulties created by this fiercely-guarded autonomy of the affiliated organisations showed themselves most clearly as soon as the Labour Government of 1945 began to try to hammer out a wages policy in consultation with the General Council. As soon as some sort of agreement had been reached between the two bodies, the General Council decided that their normal channels of contact with the affiliated unions would be insufficient to secure the acceptance of the agreement by the movement, and they therefore resorted to the device of calling meetings of the whole of the national executive committees of all the affiliated organisations. But a difference of machinery does not create a difference in relations, and these meetings turned out to be just as exhortatory in tone and just as inconclusive in effect as any other contact between the General Council and the affiliated organisations.

Many trade unionists defended, and still defend, the loose organisation of the trade union movement on the grounds that Labour government is not a permanency, and that it is necessary to preserve the fighting power of the unions against the day when the standards of their members might again be threatened by a Conservative government. This argument is erroneous, for two reasons. In the first place, the power of the unions to oppose, if need be, the government of the day is not diminished but increased if the unions have a medium through which they can speak firmly with a single voice. When trade union standards are attacked by employers and by a government acting in support of employers, the most effective form of attack has always been to play off one section of the workers against another or against the rest. The power of resistance to this form of attack would clearly be enhanced if the central organ of the movement had more jurisdiction than at present over the affiliated organisations.

Secondly, the power-relationship between the government (of any colour) and the trade union movement has changed for all time. That relationship has been revolutionised not merely by full employment, which could conceivably be brought to an end by government action, but still more by the effects of Britain's weakened economic position, which are likely to be with us for as far ahead as we can see. Since our standard of living depends on national production, and since the survival (or at least the re-election) of a government depends, in peacetime, on its defence of the standard of living, every government is heavily dependent on the goodwill of the trade union movement. It was his realisation of this dependence which led Mr. Churchill to placate the trade unions by his speeches during the 1951 General Election campaign and by his subsequent appointment as Minister of Labour of the 'neutral' Monckton instead of the 'political' Maxwell Fyfe.

Perhaps the clearest evidence of this new relationship is contained in the changed position of the trade union Member of Parliament. The sponsorship by some unions of parliamentary candidates was designed to give those unions a voice in the framing of legislation which affected their members' interests and an *entrée* to Ministers of the Crown for representations about those interests. But nowadays no legislation, or other governmental action, affecting the interests of (say) miners is, or can be, introduced into the House unless the Ministers concerned have had prior consultations with the National Union of Mineworkers. Similarly, if the National Executive of the N.U.M. wants to make representations to the Minister of Fuel and Power, it doesn't have to ask the miners' M.Ps. to go on a deputation to him: all that happens is that Sir Will Lawther rings up the Minister, goes round to see him, and is hastily and deferentially ushered in and given a cordial greeting and a cup of tea.

This new deference shown by governments, irrespective of their colour, to the trade union movement is matched by a new deference shown by capital to labour. The advent of the Conservative Government in 1951 did not lead to any diminution of the discussions about, and the first tentative moves towards, a new relationship in the private sector between the owners of the equity and the workers in the factories. Many industrialists, looking beyond short-term changes in the composition of governments, are convinced that, in the long run, they can hope to escape all-out socialisation only by a new capital-labour relationship. It is this conviction which motivates the acceptance of a greatly increased measure not merely of workers' participation in management, but also of workers' participation in the distribution of profits, through either some form of co-partnership or even a radical change in the form of the joint stock company.

Thus it is a mistake, or a rationalisation, to argue that the unions' jealous preservation of their autonomy is forced on them by external factors. Nor is it entirely (though it is to some extent) the result of a general resistance to change in any form. Principally it is the product of the structure of the movement and of the attitudes which are created by that structure.

Consider the method of election of the General Council, which consists of representatives chosen from nineteen trade sections (counting women workers as a section). In the ten sections which elect only one member each, the general secretary of the largest union in the section is virtually an automatic choice. In the remaining nine sections, for each of which more than one member is elected, the choice is made by mutual 'accommodation' between the leading unions in the section. The results of this method are, firstly, that the composition of the General Council is virtually unchanging and unchangeable, and, secondly, that the movement abounds in frustrated general secretaries who, so long as they stay with their present unions, can never get on the General Council. If they now gave up their autonomy to the General Council, they would be putting the destinies of their unions into the hands of men who in one sense are their colleagues but in another very real sense are their active rivals. When the Devil joins God on the side of the big battalions, the little squads insist on digging their own trenches.

So long as trade unions are organised on a craft-and-general rather than an industrial basis, and so long, therefore, as the majority of workers are eligible for membership of more than one union, it is inevitable that there should be some rivalry between unions. The fact that power rests, for the most part, on the block vote excites every union to increase its membership; and in many sectors of the working class it is unfortunately easier to strengthen one union at the expense of another than to convert non-unionsts to unionism.

This rivalry between unions no longer has any serious effects in direct competition in recruitment, partly because of the regulation of recruitment by the Bridlington Agreement, and partly because union organisers at field-officer level respect one another's rights. But it does have serious effects in inhibiting, or at least weakening, joint action between different unions in the same industry. In some joint industrial councils and similar bodies the larger unions sometimes squabble between themselves about the allocation of places and then unite to ensure that the smaller unions don't get any places at all. To take another example, the pursuit of a claim for higher wages for railway shopmen was for a long time held back by an open breach between the National Union of Railwaymen and the Confederation of Shipbuilding and Engineering Unions. One could quote many other examples; and perhaps the most serious result of this inter-union rivalry is that in some cases it has militated against the setting up, and effective working, of joint consultative bodies in some industries in which those bodies were most vitally needed. Something of this sort happened for a time after the nationalisation of the railways; and in some sections of cotton-weaving it is easier to get overlookers to consult with employers and weavers to consult with employers than it is to get overlookers to consult with weavers.

It should be borne in mind that inter-union rivalry is

inevitable in the present state of development of the movement, that not all of its features are unhealthy, that it is not nearly so prevalent as is sometimes pretended by anti-trade unionists, and that certainly it is microscopic compared with the overall solidarity and comradeship of the movement. But it does have the effect of making the unions unwilling to give up any of their powers to a body consisting of men and women with vested interests of their own. There can, in fact, be no hope of creating an effective central policy-making organ for the whole movement unless that organ is constituted quite differently from the present General Council.

This 'constitutional' cause of strain between various unions, and between most of the unions and the General Council, has in recent years been reinforced by a quite different cause which has the same effects—namely, the friction between communist and anti-communist union leaders and their respective organisations. Trade union officials conduct their political arguments with much less tolerance and much more bitterness than politicians ever show to one another. No Labour M.P. ever spoke about Mr. Willie Gallacher, and Mr. Gallacher never spoke about any Labour M.P., in the kind of language that communist and anti-communist trade unionists use to, and about, one another. In many cases their attitude, on both sides of the argument, has become almost pathological, and certainly it often results in a failure to consider an industrial question on its merits because of political dislike of the person, or the union, which initiated it.

So far we have considered the factors which militate against the centralisation of powers at a level above that of the individual union. But just as there are some trade union functions which require further centralisation, so there are many others which require further decentralisation to lower levels, especially the level of the factory. The fact is that there are very few functions which are best dealt with at the level of the union executive.

This condition arises because of the heterogeneous nature of

British trade unions. The 186 unions represented at the 1951 Congress varied in size from the Transport and General Workers' Union, with 1,241,787 members, to the formidably-titled National Amalgamated Association of Nut and Bolt Makers, which has nationally amalgamated and associated the whole of a mass membership of thirty. They varied in scope between those unions, like the National Union of General and Municipal Workers, which cast their membership net over almost the whole of industry, and a considerable number of unions which restrict themselves geographically or vocationally or in other ways, like the Cardiff, Penarth and Barry Coal Trimmers' Union, the Military and Orchestral Musical Instrument Makers' Trade Society, the Bedstead Workers' Association, the Huddersfield Healders' and Twisters' Trade and Friendly Society, and the London Jewish Bakers' Union. There are wide disparities in organisation and structure between different industries. Sometimes (as in coalmining) there are one predominant union and a few marginal ones; sometimes (as in agriculture) there is nominally a single industrial union, but it has to face the competition of a general union. At the other end of the scale, a small industry like airline operation, with only a few thousand workers in all, is organised by some twenty unions; and in a single motor-car factory there may be members of up to forty unions. Organised engineers and electricians are to be found predominantly in engineering and electricity, but there are always a few of them in every textile or chemical or rubber or any other non-engineering and non-electrical factory. (There are even engineers in art galleries and electricians in gasworks!) There are a few unions which are vertical and a few which are horizontal (like the general unions and some of the 'white-collar' unions); but most are an illogical mixture, in different proportions, of vertical and horizontal organisation.

That is why, as we have already said, there are very few functions which are best dealt with at the level of the union executive. Every union executive represents something different from every other union executive: one will speak for most of the workers in one industry; another for most of the workers in one industry in one area; another for many workers in one industry and a few in many other industries; another for one vocational group in one industry; another for one vocational group in all industries; and yet another for odd groups of workers in many industries. In some industries, confederations of unions have been created in an endeavour to find a more logical policy-making unit than this hotch-potch of variegated units; but whilst these confederations have removed some anomalies they have created others in their place.

Thus the great majority of union functions need to be fulfilled either at a higher level or at a lower level than that of the union executive. We have already discussed the resistances to reference upwards, but the resistances to delegation downwards are no less strong.

Over the greater part of organised labour in Great Britain, the gap between the professional union official and the lay member is widening. This is particularly serious at the present time, when serious attempts are being made to get the men in the factory to take an interest in, and to fit themselves for, workers' participation in management. The trouble is that this strain between the official and the lay member slows up the develop-ment of better industrial relationships in the better-managed firms, because the attitude of the officials is that no workers ought to make concessions to even the best of employers whilst there is a danger that a nearby bad employer will then demand the same concessions. A.E.U. shop stewards in 'good' firms, who agree with their managements about new productivity techniques, find this agreement vetoed in the district committee by shop stewards in other firms, egged on by the district official, who has the job of defending workers' standards in establishments where the industrial relations climate is bad. Similarly, in Lancashire the workers in the 'good' mills are restrained from redeploying by the workers in the bad mills, who are again encouraged in their attitude by the district official.

That official adopts this attitude for three reasons. In the first place, he is generally overworked, and therefore likes simple solutions to his problems, and particularly the simple, comfortable solution of sticking to the strict letter of a national agreement and of not incurring the headaches of local variations. Secondly, he is afraid that if he gives his shop stewards any further powers it will weaken his own prestige. (This is his subjective understanding of the wider problem that the creation of effective organs of joint consultation inevitably reduces the dependence of the worker on his union.) And, thirdly, he's afraid (and not without cause, as A.E.U. history shows) that if he gives any rope to the shop stewards they may be captured by the communists.

This gap between the lay member and the district official becomes wider between the lay member and the national official. Many unofficial strikes are not against the employers, but against the union's national executive or its national trade council. One factor intensifying this division is the growth of the joint industrial council as the bargaining-machine for a whole industry. This applies equally in both publicly-owned and privately-owned industries; but the division is intensified in the nationalised industries by the problems arising from the creation in those industries of statutory joint consultation down to the workshop level.

Let us look at the general problem first, and then go on to consider the intensification of the problem in the public sector. We can do this by considering what might happen, for example, in a joint industrial council for the furniture industry. (This is taken as a hypothetical example, and without reference to the existing J.I.C.) On the workers' side such a body would almost certainly be manned exclusively by professional trade union officers. Some (but not necessarily all) of those officers may have worked in the industry in their day, but that day was not yesterday, or even the day before. Their members know that; and if the J.I.C. reaches an agreement which the workers consider wrong, they ascribe the error (not always justly) to their representatives' ignorance of the trade as it is operated to-day. The woodcutting-machinist in a furniture factory is interested only in the wages and conditions of woodcutting-machinists in the furniture factories. But his representative on the furniture J.I.C., who knows that any wage agreement always has what are called 'repercussive effects' on all other wages, has to negotiate for his members in furniture factories with half an eye on the interests of his members in sawmills and assembly plants.

What intensifies this problem in the nationalised industries is that there the rank-and-file worker has had a taste of doing his own consultation at the factory level, often with a great deal of success, and so he is even more intolerant of the efforts at the national level of officers from outside the industry. Because he has done well in joint consultation at the workplace level, he wants to take part (himself and not by proxy) in all the joint machinery right up to the top. He is not allowed to, for the reasons we have already discussed. The result is that national consultation and local consultation are two quite separate things with very few points of contact, and the two-way channel of information between the corporation and the workers, which is the first essential of good industrial relations and the only safeguard against workers' frustration, is at best sluggish and at worst non-existent.

It is instructive to contrast this present arrangement with the theoretically ideal 'pyramid' system in consultation. Under such a system—in coal, for example—one would recruit some of the representatives on the area committee from the members of the pit committees, some of the representatives on the divisional committee in the same way from the area committees, and then some of the representatives of the national committee in the same way from the divisional committees. This would create both a channel for reporting and a chain of responsibility.

Symptoms of the friction between national and subordinate levels in consultation have been showing themselves for some time, in demands for members of the national committee to visit workplace committees, and vice versa; in demands that the national members shall consist of, or at least include, some elected rank-and-file workers; and in demands that national agreements shall not be concluded without a referendum. These demands come from the keen men who compose or follow the work of the local committees: the rest just go sour.

In each of the principal nationalisation Acts there was carefully inserted a provision that the unions must be consulted not merely on wages, working conditions, health, welfare and safety, but also on 'efficiency in the operation of the Corporation's services'. But one can't consult on this subject unless one takes the time and the trouble to study each issue as it crops up. The trade union officers do not know the issues, and have not the time to study them, or the will or means to hire people to advise them; whilst the rank-and-file workers, who do know the issues, are kept off the national committees.

It is a growing understanding by workers of this situation which contributes to a weakening of their confidence in their leaders. Another factor which contributes to the same end is the dilution of the quality of union leadership which results from the processes of 'unnatural selection' by which the best potential and actual leaders are creamed off into other *métiers*. There are four such processes: first, there is the general filtering-off of a large part of the potential working-class elite through the grammar school entry; second, some of the best young men who used to force their way to the top through the hierarchy of their union now get scholarships to the London School of Economics or Ruskin College and never go back; third, some of the best potential leaders go into parliament; and fourth, some of the best of the established leaders join the boards of public corporations.

We have already considered the ways in which the structure of the movement, and particularly the gap between the official and the lay member, inhibit the best development of joint consultation. Those conditions have two other inhibiting effects: they slow down the adoption of just and effective systems of payment by results, and they weaken the individual member's urge to participate in the day-to-day work of his branch and his union.

A system of payment by results is the one thing above all others that cannot be mass-produced in a single model for a whole industry and then applied as a strait-jacket to every separate factory. An incentive payment method for a factory has to be tailor-made to that factory's requirements after the most careful and expert study of its production, its layout and the distribution of its personnel. The present fever amongst factory managements for sticking in any old bonus scheme taken from any old text-book, without expert consideration of all the factors involved, is doing a great deal of damage. Over-sectionalised systems cause friction between the operator and the ratefixer. Systems which are purely quantitative cause friction between the operator and the inspector, or lead to a decline in quality, or both. Systems which are partial cause friction between the direct operators who get the bonus and the 'on-cost' workers who do not. Systems based on inaccurate ratefixing create 'fat' jobs and 'lean' jobs and hence friction between one operator and another. And systems which are superimposed on bad factory layout and bad production control—which are expected, in fact, to be a substitute for good management and not merely one of its tools—lower workers' morale, because they create incentive and then stop it working.

But if, by contrast, one sets out to discuss in respect of a given factory the delicately-balanced arguments between individual and group bonus, between the inclusion and exclusion of indirect workers, between 'budgetary' payments and purely quantitative payments, then such discussions cannot be undertaken by the union's national executive, or even (in any detail) by the district official, but must devolve for the most part on the workers' representatives in that particular factory. Thus, as in the case of joint consultation (of which this is, in one way, one specialised facet, though it is also something more), the adoption of modern payment methods demands a new balance and a new relationship between the lay member and the union hierarchy.

It also demands, of course, the training of shop stewards and other workers' representatives to fit them for participation in management. On this subject, all that needs to be said is that everybody agrees that this job ought to be tackled, most people are keen to tackle it, and nobody does anything much about it. The Government leaves it to the T.U.C., the T.U.C. (with one small exception) leaves it to the unions, and the unions leave it to providence. A small number of trade unionists are put through very short courses in the T.U.C. school at Clapham. The Workers' Educational Association and the Workers' Educational Trade Union Committee run lectures and courses which cannot hope to do more than scratch the surface of the subject. In some unions a small number of the members receive, at the union's expense, an occasional rudimentary correspondence course from the National Council of Labour Colleges. The General Council, and a few unions, run short and perfunctory courses which reach only a small number of people. One or two unions have had one or two of their officers trained in the narrow subject of motion and time study, but not one union has so far managed to spare even one of its officers for three months for a full course at the Administrative Staff College. There are a few inadequate courses, nearly all conducted in the evenings, run by local education authorities, but little has been done to adjust their syllabuses to the needs of organised labour. It is doubtful whether there are three unions in the whole country which spend 1s. per annum per member on education for the new role and the new responsibilities of the trade unionist.

The only other effect of the structure of the unions which we shall here consider is the effect on branch business and branch attendances. Almost all keen and thoughtful trade unionists are agreed that, irrespective of what other changes are made, any great improvement in the movement must depend on attracting a far larger proportion of its members to share the burden of its day-to-day work. In most union branches, except on the abnormal occasions when there is a row or a strike in the offing, the average attendance at branch meetings is invariably below 10% and often below 5%. Decisions are regularly made, and officers are regularly elected, by a small group of regular attenders. (That explains why, amongst other things, an organised minority group, like the Communists, can often command a majority of elective offices.) Decisions of national bodies and leaders are unintelligible to the majority of members who, because they stay away from branch meetings, do not hear the facts and the arguments motivating those decisions.

The major cause of this condition is, of course, rank-and-file apathy; but an important contributory cause is the fact that most branch meetings are deathly dull. The complex and top-heavy structure of many unions results in a flood of mimeographed circulars to branch secretaries from head office and district office, and generally these are read right through at the branch meeting, even though they may have little or no application to most of the members present, with all the seriousness of a religious rite and the monotony of a *muezzin's* cadence. It is little wonder that most workers, at the end of a day's work, find this performance less attractive than their allotment in summer and their dart-board in winter.

An attempt to extend this analysis of the problems of the trade union movement into a programme for their solution would be beyond the scope of an essay, and might, in any event, be considered an act of gross presumption if carried out by any one trade unionist, and perhaps especially by one writing as a Fabian. But it is possible to deduce from the analysis some idea of what might possibly be the next steps in trade union development.

First, the movement needs to hammer out for itself a new type of central machinery. This might well be in two tiers: (i) a General Council larger than the present one and elected by a less rigid formula which did not lead to the automatic re-election of the same members, and (ii) an inner cabinet of non-departmental ministers, i.e. of leaders who have severed their connection with their unions and serve on this cabinet full time. This inner executive would need to hire the best available advisers in all its fields of work—not least the fields of industrial organisation and management—and that would involve a radical departure from the present practice of paying trade union experts at rates much lower than those of their opposite numbers in the employers' organisations. The executive should also be prepared to co-opt freely for special purposes, and from amongst people other than overworked general secretaries and national officers.

Second, the powers of these central bodies would need to be much greater than those of the present General Council. This in turn, would involve the cession by each union of some of the constituents of its national sovereignty. Those powers would be taken up by the General Council, which in turn would delegate some of them to the executive. One can visualise that in practice the executive, because it consisted of the best people and because it was a full-time body commanding expert advice, would generally have little difficulty in getting its views accepted by the General Council.

Third, the central body should collect a levy for, initiate, and in consultation with the unions, supervise, large-scale educational programmes for both union officers and lay members.

Fourth, it should initiate machinery for devising, in each industry, a system by which the maximum possible devolution takes place from union head offices and district offices to the workshop level. One measure which would facilitate this devolution would be an increase in the organisation of union branches on a workplace rather than on a residential basis, especially in the big cities where workers, when they leave their factories, spread out over a wide area. Workplace branches are much more effective units than 'residence' branches for the purposes of both negotiation and consultation, not least because of the co-operation which is possible between branches of different unions in the same factory. This is a develpoment which a General Council with wider powers could actively foster.

Fifth, it should also encourage a programme of education in the conduct of branch business, including the filtering of routine business by the branch officers and committee, and discussion techniques, designed to attract higher attendances at branch meetings. This improvement could reasonably be expected to lead, in turn, to fuller participation by lay members in union work at higher levels.

The British trade union movement has many high qualities which are unequalled, and in some respects unapproached, by any other mass organisation anywhere in the world. In a crisis its leaders almost invariably pull out great reserves of statesmanship, and its members draw on great reserves of sound common sense. It is stable, temperate, cool-headed and responsible. It seldom fails to recognise, and reject, the shallow and the meretricious. It is indifferent equally to threats and bribes. And it discriminates carefully between its critical friends and its hostile critics.

Its defects are, to a large extent, the defects of its qualities. Its responsibility sometimes turns to caution, its stability to lethargy, its temperateness to conservatism. But there are many within its ranks, at high levels and low, who recognise that the moment has come for the next mutation in the evolutionary process. If they succeed in convincing their fellows, the trade union movement which has won its defensive and protective battle against capitalism may do equally well in the positive tasks of building the socialist commonwealth.

POWER POLITICS AND THE LABOUR PARTY

Denis Healey

THAT external factors would one day dominate British politics was never conceived by the founders of British socialism. Apart from one reference to the foreign policy of the Manchester School, the original volume of *Fabian Essays* never mentions the world outside Britain except to point a domestic moral. Indeed, this sort of parochialism was the Fabians' greatest strength. They found socialism wandering aimlessly in Cloud Cuckoo land and set it working on the gas and water problems of the nearest town or village. The modern Welfare State is their monument.

But the very success of Fabianism as an instrument of domestic reform condemns it as a guide to world politics. The world as a whole has never resembled the delicately integrated democracy which Britain developed in the three centuries following the Civil Wars—nor have more than a tiny minority of the states within it. *Leviathan* is still a better handbook for foreign policy than *Fabian Essays*.

An understanding of the power element in politics is the first necessity for a sound foreign policy. The trade union movement, as the other main contributor to British socialism, can still, as so often in the past, go some way towards filling this gap in Fabian theory. But the trade union movement is even more afflicted by parochialism, and it tends to intervene in the formation of foreign policy to correct errors rather than to give positive direction.

The major positive influences on Labour Party thinking about world affairs have come from neither the Fabians nor the trade unions, but from the liberal-Nonconformist wing with its bias towards pacifism, and the neo-Marxist wing, stemming from continental Social Democracy and Communism.

Because the Party as a whole lacks any systematic theory of

M

world affairs, it has too often fallen victim to the besetting sin of all progressive opposition movements—utopianism. In particular, it tends to discount the power element in politics, seeing it as a specific evil of the existing system rather than a generic characteristic of politics as such. The liberal utopian believes that if left to themselves men will automatically act for the common interest. The Marxist utopian exaggerates the influence of economic factors on human behaviour and believes that all social evils stem from a bad system of property relations. In both cases depreciation of the power factor entails an inadequate understanding of the techniques of power.

Conservative movements which represent the ruling class have the opposite temptation. For them the exercise of power easily becomes an end in itself and the sole aim of all political activity. In Mannheim's words: 'The Conservative type of knowledge originally is the sort of knowledge giving practical control. It consists of habitual orientations towards those factors which are immanent in the present situation.' Thus it makes obsolescent administrative techniques serve as a substitute for policy in a changing world.

The foreign policies of the British parties bear out these generalisations. The Conservatives have a congenital grasp of the rules of thumb for protecting British interests as defined in the Victorian heyday. But they are slow to recognise changes in those interests and even slower to understand changes in the world within which their rules of thumb must be applied.

The Labour Party, on the other hand, has always been more alive to change in world affairs than to continuity. It is highly sensitive to the economic factors in international life. But it tends to see power politics as a disease peculiar to capitalism and to under-estimate or misjudge the power factors in a given situation. At worst it is so little conscious of Britain's national interests that its attention can be attracted to world affairs only by high-flown formulas which quickly lose their relevance. Particularly when the Labour Party is in office, foreign policy becomes the last refuge of utopianism.

For the utopian, Heaven is always round the corner, every

evil has a single cause and thus a single cure—there is always 'One Way Only'. Socialist attitudes to war provide many examples. Esperanto has always been popular among socialists on the grounds that nations would cease to fight one another if they all spoke the same language. Though war is at least 3,000 years older than capitalism, many socialists believe that capitalism is the only cause of war, and that therefore the Soviet Union could not commit aggression because it has a 'socialist' economy. Others maintain that the only serious danger of war springs from disparities between the living standards of the peoples; yet it is difficult to find a single war in modern times which was caused primarily by such disparities.

Between the wars this type of utopianism had a damaging influence on Labour's attitude to world affairs. Despite the contribution of the two Labour Governments towards the maintenance of collective security through the League of Nations—above all in the Geneva Protocol—the first great crisis of collective security in Manchuria swept the Party into an ostrich-like policy of total war-resistance. In 1934 the trade unions forced the Party back to collective security and in 1935 Bevin led a crushing attack against the pacifism of Lansbury and the pseudo-revolutionary naïveté of the Socialist League. Yet much Labour propaganda continued pacifist in spirit right up to the outbreak of war, and the Party's attitude towards rearmament remained equivocal.

Most British socialists had been preaching for years that war was the inevitable consequence of capitalism and that no capitalist government could be trusted to use power for peaceful ends. This belief made nonsense of the Labour Party's policy for maintaining collective security through the League of Nations, which was indeed from that point of view an 'international burglars' union', as Sir Stafford Cripps maintained. But the bulk of the Party, while believing in the intrinsic wickedness of capitalism, expected capitalist states in the League to behave more altruistically than states have ever behaved in history. The League of Nations failed, as Arthur Henderson said, not because its machinery was imperfect, but because its members would not use that machinery against their own conception of their national interests. But when have states ever shown such altruism?

Parochialism also played its part. The shortcomings of British conservatism always stood between the Labour Party and the foreign scene. In the 'twenties many English socialists thought Britain more responsible than Germany for the first World War. In the 'thirties they thought the City of London responsible for Hitler. This sort of parochialism survived the second World War: in the 'fifties a Labour Party Conference cheered the statement that Churchill was responsible for Stalinism in Russia. And it is not confined to socialists in Britain: Republicans in the U.S.A. maintain that the Democratic Administration is responsible for communism in China.

These criticisms of the Labour Party's attitude to world affairs do not apply to the foreign policy of the two brief pre-war Labour Governments and still less to the post-war foreign policy of Ernest Bevin, a man with those qualities of character, judgment and imagination which go to make a great Foreign Secretary. But they are still valid for the bulk of the Party membership. Indeed, Bevin's foreign policy never obtained wholehearted approval from the more enthusiastic socialists in the Party, and many of those who did approve it believed that it was not to any significant degree a socialist policy. Thus the Party as a whole gave only reluctant support to the Government's handling of Great Power relations, though it took genuine pride in the Government's Commonwealth and Colonial policy —above all, the transfer of power in India.

There is no doubt that the Labour Government, because it was socialist, showed far more understanding and sympathy for the revolutionary trends in Asia and Africa than the Conservative opposition. That Britain is now the one white country with genuine friends in Asia is due to the speed with which power was transferred in India and the economic assistance which the new states received: both were opposed by the Conservatives. The Government showed similar understanding for the Chinese revolution, though the fruits of this policy will be slow to mature. British influence was instrumental towards changing Dutch policy towards Indonesia. It is easy to say Britain should have done more to change French policy in Indo-China in the same way, but at the critical time de Gaulle was the French Prime Minister and British relations with France were already strained over Syria.

The contrast between achievement in this sphere and the disappointment in the wider field of world affairs is not, however, due to a sudden failure of socialist principle in dealing with power politics, for in its handling of the post-war situation the Labour Government showed both an understanding and a moral strength which owed much to socialist conviction.

The essence of British socialism lies not in its contingent analysis or techniques, but in its determination to apply moral principles to social life. It belongs to that stream of Christian thought which, while insisting that the individual human personality is an end in itself—indeed the only temporal end in itself—believes that all men are brothers, and must realise their brotherhood in this world by creating a society in which they enjoy an equal right and duty to freedom and responsibility. It is in this sense that our socialism is inseparable from democracy.

As a political programme, socialism developed during the nineteenth century in a number of industrialised European democracies as a protest against economic conditions which prevented working men from enjoying the freedom Liberalism claimed to have won for them in the political field. The analysis it made of those economic conditions and the techniques it invented to change them are still relevant to societies which resemble the industrial capitalist democracies of the nineteenth century, but elsewhere they have less guidance to offer. Confronted by modern American capitalism or by primitive peasant societies, socialists must make a new analysis and develop new techniques by which to fulfil their moral principles. This is even more necessary in dealing with the affairs of the world as a whole.

By choosing the phrase 'Social Democracy' to distinguish

their policy from that of other parties, socialists assume that society has already realised political democracy. But in world affairs the political foundations on which the theory of Social Democracy is built have yet to be laid. Indeed the basic problem which socialists face in the world as a whole is almost the opposite of that which they have hitherto faced in national societies. Instead of adjusting the economic system to realise a community already established in the political field, they must adjust political relations to realise a community already existing in the technological field. They must build a world society before they can build a socialist world.

The problem is primarily political, not economic or social. It concerns the acquisition, organisation and distribution of power. Power is not, of course, the only reality in world affairs. But it is a pervasive reality which has its own laws and fixes the limits within which moral criteria can operate. The central problem of politics arises from the fact that every time a political entity grows in size, strength or solidarity, it tends to obscure the fundamental brotherhood of its members with the members of other entities and thus to license immoral behaviour towards them. *Un bon père de famille est capable de tout.* 'If we had done for ourselves what we have done for Italy,' said Cavour, 'what scoundrels we would have been.'

In foreign as in domestic affairs, socialists should aim at changing the existing system so as to realise the fundamental brotherhood of all men and to check the selfish will to power. It is a fact that power tends to corrupt, but it is also a fact that men and even governments may resist corruption without sacrificing power. The urge to brotherhood is no less real a political fact than the will to power. In social as in personal life, moral progress is possible, although it is not automatic. Here the socialist stands midway between the liberal optimist and the conservative pessimist. In domestic affairs, since socialists already operate within a framework of law, they can make the necessary changes by consent through legislation. But in world affairs law is rarely able to override power and power is frequently exercised in its crudest form as physical force.

Many socialists believe that the political entities from which a world society must be built are social classes or political movements extending across the frontiers of nation states. This belief has always been a basic principle of Communist theory. It was Sir Stafford Cripps' reason for opposing sanctions against Italy in 1935. It often appeared in Labour criticism of Bevin's foreign policy.

In fact, however, the world has so long been divided into geographical units, each developing at a different rate and in a different direction, that there is little basis of interest or sentiment to unite classes occupying roughly similar positions in the social pattern of their various states.

The industrial proletariat, to which this theory is usually applied, is comparatively unimportant except in Western Europe and the United States of America. Even where the proletariat is a major element in its nation state, it does not automatically agree either in theory or practice with the proletariat of other states—still less with the peasant population of its own state.

Though the majority of workers in Britain and Scandinavia support socialism, their comrades in France and Italy are Communists, while in North America they believe in free enterprise capitalism. In Argentina they form the backbone of General Peron's dictatorship. Further disagreements appear on practical problems. Italian and Polish miners can testify that trade unionists are as anxious as employers to protect their livelihood from foreign competition. The Lancashire textile worker joins the Lancashire mill-owner in opposing the common interests of textile workers and employers in Japan. Thus the popular injunction to side in all cases with the workers is no guide to foreign policy.

A policy based on socialist solidarity is still more difficult to apply. Democratic socialism is even less widespread and powerful than trade unionism and even more coloured by national interests. Every democratic socialist party aims primarily at achieving power in its own nation state and is thus obliged to consider the interests of its own state first. Indeed, to the extent that the internal structure of a given state satisfies the need of the workers within it, to that extent its socialist party will tend to put the national interest before international solidarity. It is no accident that in their approach to European unity since 1945 the socialist parties of Britain and Scandinavia have been most conservative—for they have most to conserve. Economic factors reinforce the trend towards nationalism in a governing socialist party: in a world predominantly capitalist, national economic planning may often be inconsistent with forms of international co-operation a *laisser-faire* government would be quite willing to accept.

The fact is that the nation state is by far the most important political entity in world affairs. Nationalism is the one force strong enough to defeat all comers, whether the imperialism of the past or the totalitarianism of the present.

Many British socialists share the liberal belief that every nation state is a moral entity with natural rights and duties which are ultimately compatible with the rights and duties of other nation states. But nation states are political entities, not moral entities; with interests and desires, not rights and duties. Liberal theory gives all states the right to security. But the security of Russia's western frontier is incompatible with the security of Germany's eastern frontier, and both Russia's security and Germany's security are incompatible with the existence of Poland as a nation state.

The relations of nation states are determined primarily by their power to pursue their interests, and they usually conceive their interests in narrowly selfish terms. The influence of a British Labour Government in world affairs will in the first place depend on the power at its command and on the skill with which it uses that power. What then is the most hopeful path towards a world society?

Orthodox Labour theory maintains that a world society can best be created by establishing the rule of law through a universal organisation like the League of Nations or the United Nations; within this general framework of international order nations can be brought into closer and more lasting co-operation through regional or functional institutions like OEEC or the Atlantic Pact.

At the present time international order is at once more necessary and more difficult to establish than ever before. Modern technology has both united and shrunk the world. Nation states are becoming ever stronger and closer to one another. Events in one part of the world immediately affect power relationships in all other parts. In particular, any local war may develop rapidly into a world war in which new weapons of mass destruction threaten even the survival of the human race. All states have—and recognise—a powerful common interest in preventing war and economic crisis.

On the other hand, many parts of the world are undergoing revolutionary changes on a scale which occurs only once in a millennium. In non-Communist Asia and Africa, the peoples are growing faster than their food production. They are demanding at once national independence, freedom from white control and a rapid rise in living standards. The rest of Asia and Eastern Europe is organised under a totalitarian regime which believes itself destined to rule the world. The United States of America, economically the most powerful of all countries, has leapt in a few years from isolationism to active participation in world affairs.

Socialists are by nature sensitive to these changes, as the Labour Government's policy in Asia has proved. Here too, however, the besetting sin of utopianism is always offering its temptations. Too often socialists tend to imagine that changes are morally or practically desirable simply because they are changes. Men reared in the doctrine of automatic progress cannot help feeling that everything that will be will be right. But most historical changes are morally neutral. It is difficult to maintain that the brotherhood of men is better realised in Eastern Europe under a 'people's democracy' than it was under the Austro-Hungarian Empire.

Moreover, those who imagine they are jumping on the bandwagon of history often find that they have chosen the wrong vehicle. The world is going through profound changes, but it is difficult to interpret these changes rightly and impossible to predict their outcome. Many of the visible trends contradict one another. The century of the common man is also the era of the rape of the masses and of the managerial revolution. If economic man is dead in Europe he is deified in America. Most European interpretations are wrong because they use terms derived from Europe's own experience in the last hundred years. Not only the Webbs in 1935 but even Professor Carr in 1951 can describe Soviet Communism in terms of nineteenth-century European trends towards economic planning. But the striking thing about the world revolution is that everywhere the differences from European precedent are more important than the similarities. European categories crumble when applied to what is going on in Asia, Russia, and America. The same slump which produced Hitler in Europe produced Roosevelt in the U.S.A. Keynesian economics does not explain the problem of unemployment in India.

While these great changes are still in progress there is a danger in creating international institutions which attempt to set a rigid pattern for relations between the powers. Unless international institutions allow for major changes, they will not only break down, but even increase the danger of world conflict. The juridical approach to international affairs is especially dangerous, since international law reflects a pattern of power which is changing daily. An international system must be founded on recognised common interests or a stable pattern of power—or both. It may then develop habits of co-operation which enable it to survive when the basis of interest or power has disappeared. But the development of common interests or the establishment of a stable power pattern must precede and not follow the creation of rigid legal or institutional forms.

The United Nations Assembly, for example, has assumed a universal authority, although decisions may be taken by a majority of states with little knowledge of or interest in the issues at stake and representing a minority both of people and of power. By its handling of the problems posed by Chinese intervention in the Korean war, the United Nations has already weakened its prestige throughout Asia. On the other hand, when Britain asked the Security Council to uphold her rights in Persia under international law, the majority of countries were not prepared to support international law in a case which seemed contrary to their sense of justice and history. By claiming a type of authority it is unable to exercise, the United Nations risks discrediting the very idea of international order.

One way out of the dilemma is to create regional institutions linking countries which are likely to have a continuing common interest however the major changes in the world develop. This is a wise course for small states which cannot hope separately to influence world affairs. But it carries dangers for a world power like Britain, which needs close co-operation with states in every region. For regional groups can exist only by discrimination against states outside their region. A regional federation does not necessarily contribute towards the creation of a world society. Indeed, the most dangerous conflicts in the world at present lie primarily between the two great continental federations, the United States of America and the U.S.S.R. The Commonwealth is the exception which proves this rule. Membership of the Commonwealth does not limit co-operation with states outside it precisely because the Commonwealth has no separate institutions.

Throughout its period of office, the Labour Government was severly handicapped by the absolute and relative decline in Britain's power. Peace found the ruins of Britain's nineteenth-century *imperium* strewn throughout a power vacuum which was flanked by two jealous continental super-states, each immensely stronger than before the war. But for the first few years Britain's weakness was masked by the prestige of victory, by the even greater decline of other European states, by Russia's exhaustion, and by America's readiness to accept Britain's advice until she found her feet. Thus, though even Britain's survival as an independent state was in jeopardy, the skill, patience and understanding of the Labour Government made British foreign policy the main constructive element in world affairs. And it was largely British statesmanship which not only carried the world through the emergencies of the post-war crisis, but also laid some foundations for a lasting world order.

The period of Bevin's main achievement was pre-eminently the period of the Big Three, a trinity to which Britain belonged more by prestige and diplomatic skill than by right of power.

Bevin saw immediately that the power vacuum between Russia and the U.S.A. presented the Soviet rulers with opportunities for expansion which if taken would make a third world war inevitable. He had become familiar with Communist aims and techniques in the course of his trade union life— the gibe that he thought the Soviet Union a break-away from the Transport and General Workers' Union had that element of truth. But he never allowed this to obscure his appraisal of Russia's interests as a state, and he understood far better than most what dangers would follow a failure of the Big Three to create a lasting framework of co-operation while they were still the only world powers of consequence.

Filling the power vacuum by economic aid and political integration was a prime aim of his policy. For a time he believed that Britain, as the only remaining power in the vacuum, might organise it into a third force based on co-operation between Western Europe and the Commonwealth. But experience soon showed that the vacuum could not achieve either economic recovery or military security without prolonged support from the U.S.A. Bevin's greatest personal contribution was in helping to guide America's entry into the power vacuum and in resisting Soviet expansion—largely by diplomatic bluff—until America was firmly committed there. Indeed, his achievement in peace from 1945 to 1948 was comparable with Churchill's in war from 1940 to 1941.

The techniques by which he helped to build the necessary unity against Soviet expansion—and his failures in this field, above all in the Middle East—are too well known to need recounting here. Indeed, Bevin's very achievement has encouraged the belief that in the years ahead all that is required of a Labour Foreign Secretary is to continue Bevin's work along the lines he himself set down.

In particular, the Cold War is so prominent in popular imagination that many people see the future problem essentially as to build unity throughout the 'free', i.e. non-Stalinist, world against Soviet expansion. The conventional stereotype is somewhat as follows: the rearmament of the NATO powers, extended to cover the Middle East as well as Europe, will safeguard the frontiers of the free world against direct military aggression. The only remaining problem in world affairs will then be to protect the free world against subversion from within. Stalinist policy will aim at splitting the capitalist world by exploiting its three inherent contradictions: the conflict between classes within each state, the conflict between the imperialist states and the colonial peoples they exploit, and the economic and political conflicts among the imperialist states themselves—in particular between the victors and vanquished in the World War. In order to maintain unity in the free world against Stalinist subversion, the conflict between classes must be ended by social reform: the conflict between the rich white industrialised peoples of the Atlantic community and the poor coloured peasant peoples of Asia and Africa must be ended by the grant of freedom and economic aid. Internal rivalry beween the non-Stalinist powers must be ended by the development of functional co-operation through organs such as OEEC and the Atlantic Pact. This picture is particularly attractive to British socialists since every element in it is consonant with socialist tradition, and Britain is well equipped to play the central part, since the Commonwealth spans the continents and Britain is a key member of both the Atlantic and the European communities.

In 1950 the Labour Party launched as the central element in its foreign policy the concept of a World Plan for Mutual Aid. The idea of raising living standards in the under-developed areas appeals to one of the strongest elements in socialist idealism. It is indeed the twentieth-century version of the

White Man's Burden. But besides being most desirable for moral reasons, it might help to solve many political and economic problems of the world revolution.

By raising living standards in the under-developed areas— in itself most desirable for moral and political reasons—it would expand purchasing power to match the immense increase in the world's industrial productivity and so help to bridge the gaps in international trade. For many years most of the West European countries will need more dollars than they can earn by direct exports to the dollar area. It is far better that they should earn dollars by selling equipment to Asia and Africa than receive dollars as gifts from the U.S.A. If America gave the under-developed areas dollars to spend in offshore purchases of capital goods in Europe, every dollar would do twice the work it did under Marshall Aid. Moreover, when Japanese and German production is injected into the stream of world trade, cut-throat competition will wreck the nascent political unity of the 'free world' unless markets can be expanded by some such method. Finally, the terms of trade will continue to worsen for Britain unless primary production increases to keep pace with the rise of population in Africa and Asia. Britain has thus strong reasons of national interest to urge international investment in the under-developed areas.

This general picture of a socialist foreign policy for Britain, besides its obvious appeal to socialist idealism, is closely adapted to the power realities of the present time. But unfortunately the present pattern of power relations is about to undergo important changes and some of the assumptions of the theory are at variance with the facts.

In the first place, the policies of welfare socialism as applied with such success in Britain and Scandinavia demand a level of civic responsibility and administrative competence which scarcely exists outside the Anglo-Saxon world and Northern Europe. Under British socialism the Welfare State is achieved by fiscal methods. This presumes that on the whole citizens are prepared to pay taxes and that the state machinery is efficient and honest enough to prevent tax evasion and to administer great funds successfully. This has not been the case in many parts of Europe. Most of the techniques of physical planning and control which Britain has developed during and since the war break down in a country like France, where most people see neither duty nor interest in obeying the government.

What is true of Southern Europe is even more true of Asia and Africa. And if the methods of British socialism are unable to produce social justice in many parts of the world, those of American capitalism are even less appropriate. The buoyant psychology of American business has few parallels outside the U.S.A., as the Marshall Aid administration soon discovered. The economic pre-conditions of rapid capital accumulation do not exist anywhere in Asia or Africa. There is no reason to believe that social justice in the under-developed areas will be built by British or American methods—if it is built at all.

In the second place, when the peoples of Asia and Africa win freedom from white control they will not necessarily cease to conflict with the white countries or with one another. All the problems of power politics which have tormented Europe for the last 600 years will then arise anew. It is already obvious that some of the new Asian states do not wish to take sides in the Cold War—the Stalinist bloc has at least as good a chance of winning their support as the democratic bloc. On the democratic side the Commonwealth is one of the most favourable factors. But South Africa's native policy is already incompatible with British policy in the African colonies and may soon become incompatible with keeping the Asian states in the Commonwealth.

The World Plan for Mutual Aid is impeccable in aim and general conception. But the difficulties of carrying it out will be immense. The scale of outside investment required to raise standards of living in the under-developed areas is far beyond the capacity of any combination of countries which excludes the United States. A United Nations report in 1951 estimates that an annual rise of 2% in the standard of living would require an annual investment of £3,800 million pounds. Moreover, the political and administrative problems of ensuring that the money is well spent are quite as formidable as the problem of obtaining the money from America. In any case it is doubtful whether an annual rise of 2% in the standard of living would by itself win Asia and Africa to the Western side. All these difficulties are no argument against doing what can be done in this direction. Every pound or dollar spent can mean the alleviation of some human misery. But the disillusion will be catastrophic if exaggerated expectations are aroused.

Most important of all, the pattern of power politics in the period ahead will differ greatly from that of the last six years. British influence was predominant in the non-Stalinist world immediately after the war because Britain was the only power in the power vacuum and the United States was sinking back into an isolationism tempered by large-scale welfare activity. From 1947 onwards, when America began to use her power in Europe and other parts of the vacuum, she did so mainly as a result of British diplomacy, and her policies were fully compatible if not identical with Britain's. Except in Palestine, every American irruption into Eurasian affairs up to the middle of 1950 was co-ordinated with British policy.

The Korean war brought a fundamental change in the nature of American intervention. America provided 90% of the United Nations' forces in Korea—over a quarter of a million men—and suffered heavy casualties. The average American citizen came to realise for the first time that his personal future was at stake in what the Administration was doing abroad. Congress began to interfere more energetically in the formation of foreign policy. The fact that America's prime interest in Eurasian affairs is strategic rather than political or economic, together with the exigencies of party warfare in the United States, shifted the decisive influence on policy-making from the State Department to the Pentagon. The internal impact of rearmament, far greater than that of the earlier foreign welfare programmes like Marshall Aid, meant that ordinary Americans became fully conscious of the immense power their country wielded and increasingly intolerant of foreign criticism of the way they used it.

Many English socialists are watching this development with a gloom fortified by national jealousy or doctrinal suspicion. Some take the view that Britain should withhold co-operation unless her views are met, on the grounds that she is indispensable to America's foreign policy. But while America is growing in strength and independence new powers are arising inside the vacuum created by the war. Germany in Europe and Japan in the Far East offer the American strategists additional if not alternative bases for their policy in Eurasia. The fact is that even as Britain's absolute strength is growing, her bargaining power with the United States is dwindling.

The rise of Germany and Japan may change the nature of the Cold War. The point may come at which the Soviet Union will have to decide whether to seek agreement with Britain and America to protect herself from Germany and Japan or with Germany and Japan to further her designs against Britain and America. It is too soon to feel confident that Germany and Japan will feel a strong moral obligation or material interest to side with the Atlantic powers if Russia offers them tempting concessions. Indeed, Russia has far more to offer Germany than the West—not only trade, but also political unity, including if necessary the return of the territories lost to Poland.

Germany remains the most dangerous problem for British policy in future. Britain cannot ignore the possibility that Germany may seek national unity either by war with Russia or by alliance with Russia. It has been fashionable to see the answer in integrating Western Germany into some form of West European union. Britain herself has been unwilling to join such a union for fear of losing her independence outside Europe. But it is already obvious that if European unity is built without Britain it will be dominated by Germany. As Germany revives Britain may be compelled to integrate herself more deeply with Europe than is compatible with her other economic and political interests. Indeed, America is the only state with sufficient power to spare for correcting the balance in Western Europe. But many Americans believe that Germany's revival would justify their withdrawal from Europe instead of

177

requiring them to play a more active part in Europe themselves.

Relations with the United States have thus become the central problem of British foreign policy. But material and moral factors severely limit the range of choice. Strategically Britain needs America even more than America needs Britain. Economically, though Britain might dispense with direct American aid at home, her plans for economic development abroad demand large-scale dollar aid. Politically, America's interests are far closer to those of Britain than the interests of any other present or potential ally; indeed, the Commonwealth would not survive a rupture between Britain and the U.S.A. Morally, as a progressive democracy America is far closer to Britain than is Western Europe, southern Asia, or, of course, the Soviet Union. Anglo-American unity is indeed a condition of Britain's survival.

The final major change in the post-war pattern of power-politics may come through a disruption of the Stalinist bloc. Tito's defection was premature in the sense that Russia has probably been able to eliminate the main sources of Titoism in the rest of Eastern Europe before the world situation gave them a chance of success. But the present alliance between the Soviet Union and Communist China is based on a very temporary congruence of interest. On the other hand, if China does separate herself from the Soviet Union a settlement in Eastern Asia will not necessarily become much simpler.

One thing at least is certain. The situation of 1945–50, in which the Labour Party's foreign policy came of age, has gone for good. Too many minds are still dominated by the picture of two continental super-states glowering at each other over a power vacuum in which Britain is the only strong state. The emergence of Germany, Japan and China as independent powers has already changed that picture. Within a few years southern Asia, the Middle East and Africa may also take the stage in their own right. Thus the vision of a world shaped almost exclusively by Anglo-Saxon policy is fading at the very moment when it seems most likely to become reality. It is much more probable that the future will bring a return to a world of many powers in which decisions are made by the methods of traditional power politics. If this is so, conventional diplomacy will come into its own again and the adjustment of national differences by negotiation and compromise will become more urgent than the construction of international institutions or the execution of moral blueprints.

These suggestions are offered without excessive confidence. The known facts are always so small a proportion of total reality that the fruits of scientific method should never be taken as rational grounds for defeatism or over-confidence. Three predictions at least are fairly safe. Britain's influence on world affairs in the immediate future will depend more than ever on her material power to help a friend or harm an enemy. Britain's fundamental interest in unity with the United States will remain supreme. And an understanding of power politics will be more than ever necessarry to a successful socialist foreign policy.

TASKS AND ACHIEVEMENT OF BRITISH LABOUR

John Strachey

Part I

WHAT is the extent and character of the social transformation brought about by the Labour Government in
Britain? Has the internal structure of British capitalism been
sensibly modified? In particular, has the *internal* unbalance, as
between different social groups and interest been in any way
redressed, and if so what have been the economic consequences?
These are the questions which the first part of this essay seeks
to answer.

It was always a commonplace of orthodox socialist thought
that capitalism could solve its problems if it could do two
things: if it could devote its ever-growing productivity to
raising the standard of life of the population as a whole, and
if, partly consequentially, it could develop agriculture, rousing
agriculture from its long period of comparative technical torpor.
For if these two things could be done, the main difficulties of
the system need not necessarily arise. We should no longer be
confronted with its recurrent inability to dispose of its products:
there would be no need for periodic gluts, slumps and crises, nor
for semi-chronic stagnation. And freedom from these internal
morbid symptoms would in turn remove the pressure on the
system at all costs to seek overseas markets for its surplus
products: moreover, the old necessity to export, not only
commodities, but above all capital, which could not be used
at home, would disappear: consequently, the pressure to
monopolise at all costs overseas markets and fields of investment

would be removed. And it is that pressure which socialists have always seen as the main underlying cause of modern war.

Orthodox socialists have, however, held that these things could not in fact be done under capitalism: for in order to do them policies would have to be adopted which entailed accepting a lower rate of profit than that obtainable by adhering to the traditional policies of the system. And this, it was held, capitalism, almost by definition, could not do. For it was a system of which the essence was that it followed the attraction of profit and the repulsion of loss, and in this found its one indispensable principle of regulation. Hence it was unthinkable that it should actually begin to pursue courses which entailed deliberately accepting lower rather than higher rates of profit: if it did so, it would in fact no longer be capitalism.

This was my own view until about 1938. About 1938 I began to modify these views. It was the work of a new school of economists—notably, of course, Keynes' General Theory, but also works like Douglas Jay's *The Socialist Case*—which affected my mind. And I set out my revised views in detail in a book called *A Programme for Progress*, which was published in 1940. Incidentally, the programme set out in that book is a much less far-reaching programme than the one which the Labour Government has actually carried out in the last six years. But in these matters an ounce of experience is worth a ton of theory. And it is the experience of the Labour Government which provides us with the first important evidence that much more is possible in this field than had been supposed. For in my opinion the Labour Government between 1945 and 1951 did in fact appreciably modify the nature of British capitalism.

The best test of that is, surely, afforded by observing whether or not British capitalism is still producing those intractable problems with which we were so painfully familiar before the war. For if British capitalism has in fact been modified in its basic nature during the past six years, we shall expect to find that the political and social problems with which we are now confronted are of a different—and perhaps even an opposite—kind. Let us recall for a moment what the old problems were and see whether or not they persist to-day.

The most painful of all our social problems before the war was mass unemployment: the inability of the system to employ a significant part of the available labour force. What has happened to this chronic excess of the supply of labour over the demand for it? As we all know, it has disappeared from the social scene and has in fact turned into a chronic excess of the demand for labour over its supply. Contrary to many people's impression the level of unemployment is still lower (December 1951) than it was for instance, in January 1950. Nor has this chronic labour shortage been, as is sometimes now suggested, a consequence of rearmament. It was almost as marked in 1948, 1949, and the first half of 1950 as it is to-day. Indeed it has been vigorously held that rearmament, by giving rise to a shortage of raw materials, might endanger, instead of promoting, full employment.

A second morbid symptom of our pre-war system was its inability to find employment for all our available savings and capital; the chronic, if always abortive, tendency of savings to exceed investment—no doubt the economists would tell us that this was the same symptom as mass unemployment seen from a different angle. What has happened here?

In this case again we are now faced with the opposite problem. In spite of the fact that we are now saving more than before the war, there are never enough savings to provide for all the new objects of investment which are clamouring for execution. In the Labour Government, I took part annually with my colleagues in laborious efforts to reduce our home investment programme to manageable proportions. Our national savings have on the whole been made in new ways— out of corporate, undistributed profits and out of a large Budget surplus. But in sum, they have been, I repeat, on the whole larger rather than smaller than before the war. In fact, we have probably been saving and investing a higher proportion of the national income in these past six years than for a long time. Nevertheless, there have never been enough resources saved to cover all the projects which either private firms or public corporations or Government departments ardently wished to put in hand immediately. If we had re-equipped all the mines and railways, and built all the power stations, factories, ships, houses, schools, hospitals, etc., which Government departments, public corporations and private firms alike demanded to build, we should have had hardly any resources left to live on! A drastic pruning has had to be undertaken every year. There has been no trace of the old malignant disease of under-investment. Once again symptoms of chronic stagnation have turned into symptoms of only too buoyant activity.

A third symptom of the pre-war system was its inability to find adequate overseas markets for our exports—whether of commodities or of capital. British industry could have produced many more goods for export; British investors would have been glad to place considerably greater amounts of capital overseas; outlets for neither appeared to exist. To-day there is no difficulty in finding the markets for our exports: the difficulty is to spare for export commodities for which the home market is clamouring. Again, there are hundreds of projects of overseas development for which British capital is desperately needed. The trouble is to spare any from the large home investment programme which we all agree in wishing to execute.

As a direct result of this reversal of the economic situation there has been a relaxation of the old familiar pressure to keep for ourselves what opportunities for overseas investment did arise—a relaxation of the pressure to *monopolise* overseas markets for commodities and capital. Indeed, this pressure has in some respects disappeared altogether. During the past six years the greater part of the British Empire has become independent, either within or without the Commonwealth—I wonder if either we or our opponents always realise that tremendous fact. Nevertheless, this world-shaking development has taken place, and yet none of those dire predictions as to catastrophic economic effects upon us have been fulfilled. 'Lose India', we were told, 'and half Lancashire will be unemployed.' On the contrary, India has become independent and Lancashire, which *was* half unemployed, was working all out during the whole period of the Labour Government.

In general, far from wanting to prevent other countries from providing capital or even commodities to the undeveloped areas of the world, we are now only too thankful if they will shoulder the major part of what is now seen as the immense *burden* of developing the vast under-industrialised continents of Asia and Africa.

Fourth, amidst the general tendency to stagnation which marked the economy as a whole, the tendency for British agriculture to stagnate was especially marked. There is not the slightest sign of this symptom to-day. On the contrary, we appear to be in the midst of a veritable agricultural revolution, comparable in speed and intensity to the most turbulent periods of the Industrial Revolution. The mechanisation of agricultural processes is at last going forward on a really great scale both at home and overseas.

In these four major respects, therefore, our economy is exhibiting behaviour quite different from that which it exhibited during the whole of the inter-war period. I have deliberately left out of account the question of boom and slump—of the trade cycle—since it may be argued that it is as yet too early to claim that we have succeeded in eliminating cyclical depressions. But the above comparisons hold good even if we compare our economy's performance over the past six years with its performance at the crests of the inter-war booms— with 1929 and 1937, for instance. Even on this basis there can be no denying the striking contrast between its relative stagnation then, and its extreme stimulation—some would say over-stimulation—now.

We may summarise the main figures, pointing this contrast between a rapidly expanding economy—indeed an uncomfortably rapidly expanding economy—now, and a semi-stagnant economy then, as follows:

	1938	*1950*
Electricity generated (million kilowatt-hours)	24[1]	55
Steel Ingots and castings (millions of tons)	10	16
Passenger cars (thousands) . .	341	522
Tractors (thousands) . . .	10	120
Exports (volume index, 1939 = 100) .	100	162
Industrial production all industries (1946 = 100)	100[2]	140
Unemployed	1,700,000	274,000

The question we have to ask is what has been done to the old, staid—indeed stagnant—British economy to make it behave in this way? Was it really the measures of the Labour Government which wrought this remarkable change? And if so, which measures?

In attempting to answer this question we should at the outset notice that it is not the British economy alone which has begun to behave in this new way. Several other of the larger capitalist nations show a comparable change in the behaviour of their economies. It is especially important to notice that the economy of the United States is decidedly one of these. Here are some comparable figures from the United States.

	1938	*1950*
Electricity generated (million kilowatt-hours)	114	329
Steel (Ingots and sheet for castings) (million metric tons) . . .	29	88
Passenger cars (millions) . . .	2	7
Exports (1938 = 100)	100	179
Industrial production all industries (1937 = 100)	79	177
Unemployed	10,390,000	3,142,000

(Source: *UN Monthly Bulletin of Statistics*, July, 1951.)

[1] Figures to the nearest million. (Source: *Statistical Digest*, February, 1951.)
[2] It is the statistician's best guess that 1938 was the same as 1946.

In my opinion, what originally produced these remarkable effects in America was a combination of the pre-war measures of the New Deal with the immense stimulus of war production. And then in the past six years the continuance of New Deal and Fair Deal measures have sufficed to prevent the economy dropping back into that semi-stagnation to which it had become as prone as our own. Of all the measures of the two 'Deals'—New and Fair—we may pick out as the ones which have had decisive economic effects: first, the appreciable redistribution of the national income by a much more progressive system of taxation than had ever existed before in America; and, second—and perhaps even more important—the measures by which agricultural prices have been taken right out of the free market system and largely fixed by statute.

The first conclusion to be drawn from these figures is that the extreme buoyancy of the British economy cannot be wholly attributed to the *particular* reforms of the British Labour Government. American experience shows that it is possible to produce the same results by different measures and methods—*so long as those measures add up to a real change in the balance of the social system.* Our nationalisation measures, for example, have been foundation stones for building a new type of economy permanently suitable for the modern world. But it would be wrong to claim for them that they, in themselves, have produced the extraordinary stimulation of the economy. No, we must look deeper than that for the causes of what has happened. I have no doubt that the real cause of the re-animation of the British economy lies in the shift of political power and influence between social groups which has taken place in Britain. This shift of power has expressed itself financially in a redistribution of the national income. This redistribution has as yet been limited in extent, but it has sufficed for the specific purpose of releasing the forces of production. The extent of redistribution may be indicated by the following figures.[1] Before the war the share of the national income going to rent, interest and profit, etc., was 37%; by 1950 it had fallen, after taxes had been paid, to 25%.

[1] See Command Paper 8,203.

Similarly the share going to wages was, before the war, 37%; in 1950, after tax, it had risen to 47%. But this is a narrowly financial way of putting the issue. In one sense the exact extent of the redistribution at any given moment is not the essential thing. In one sense, what is essential is that the distribution of the national income has ceased to be a largely automatic function of the way economy works—of the play of the profit motive—and has become something which is consciously, politically settled by the community's own decisions. That is itself a revolution.

Here then is my first conclusion. What all these figures indicate is that British capitalism *has* been compelled, by the sheer pressure of the British people, acting through our effective democratic political institutions, to do what we used to say it would never, by definition, do. It has been forced to devote its productive resources to raising the standard of life of the population as a whole and of developing agriculture in particular. Moreover—and whether we, or they, admit it or not—this shift in the balance of social forces has occurred, though to a lesser degree and in a different way, in America also. In America the long rule of the Democratic Party, under Roosevelt and Truman, has done one fundamental thing for the American industrial workers and one fundamental thing for the American farmers. It has enabled the American workers at length to establish solid, large and, it is now safe to say, indestructible trade unions. And it has given the American farmers relatively fixed prices for their products, thus effectively protecting them from the slumps to which they are peculiarly vulnerable. These two profound developments have, in my opinion, changed the balance of social forces in America almost to a comparable extent, though in a different way, to the change that has taken place in Britain.

In general, the grip of the major central monopoly capitalists on the economy has been, not indeed removed, but appreciably loosened in each country. And this has been sufficient to release very great productive forces—to produce in fact the remarkable economic re-animation which the figures I have given illustrate.

What should be our political conclusion from these, so far as I can see, incontrovertible economic facts? Are we not driven to the conclusion that it *is* possible in favourable circumstances for the popular forces, *if they possess well-developed and effective democratic* institutions, to drive contemporary capitalism out of its normal channels of development, to devote its vast productive energies to raising the standard of life of its own population instead of taking the fatal course of stagnation at home qualified by imperialist expansion abroad—the course which can lead to nothing but recurrent war?

Hence everything turns on the effectiveness of democracy—in the simple sense of the existence of representative governments which can be made genuinely responsive to the wants of the population. Moreover, everything turns not only on the formal existence of such democratic institutions, *but on the ability of the people to use them effectively*. Everything turns not only, that is to say, on the existence of free elections, but also, and at least equally, on the existence of a politically mature electorate and of effective and united popular political parties, capable of sustaining governments of the left. Otherwise, the popular effort will be dissipated and frustrated.

And then, of course, there is one more indispensable condition for success. The governments of the left when installed must know *how* to give effect to the push of the democratic forces. They must possess an economic *technique* for releasing the productive powers of the system and turning its energies towards the task of raising the general standard of life. What happens when such a government possesses no such economic technique is illustrated by the failure of M. Blum's Popular Front Government in France in the nineteen-thirties. This Government satisfied most of the other conditions, but it simply did not know how to make the wheels of the economic system go round. One cannot altogether blame the Blum Government for this; a worse case still is afforded of course by the British Labour Government of 1929-31. The techniques for making an economic system work at full power—granted one has the will to do so—were in fact only worked out in the nineteen-thirties. The elucidations of the late Lord Keynes have in this respect played a genuine historical role. But we must not forget that several young socialist economists also made notable contributions. Between them all they have shown *how* a government can, if it wants to, set the wheels going at full speed. Nevertheless, the major factor must always be the shift in social and political power by which alone forces which even *want* to run the economy at full speed may come to the controls. Without that shift of power no mere economic technique can have any effect.

The above picture of the British economy, as buoyant and reanimated to a degree unknown for several decades, is, I suggest, incontrovertibly true on the figures. But it is different indeed from the picture of our economy diurnally presented to us by the spokesmen of the political forces and parties of the right. They describe the British economy, for example, as 'bound and shackled' by disastrous controls and penal taxation at home, 'staggering from crisis to crisis' and 'living on foreign charity' in its external economic relations. It is, of course, perfectly natural that those who speak for the social interests which the pre-war condition of things suited far better than do our present arrangements should emphasise the negative aspects of the existing situation: it would be very odd if they did not; while we, equally naturally, emphasise the positive aspects. But there is really nothing essentially contradictory about the two accounts. The same phenomena are being observed, but from an opposite point of view. For clearly if you attempt, as we did, at one and the same time—

(*a*) to eliminate gross want from the population—and if you succeed in doing so to the remarkable extent now revealed by Mr. Rowntree in his *Poverty and the Welfare State;*
(*b*) to eliminate the major economic hazards of working-class life—unemployment, sickness, old age—by the first really comprehensive system of social insurances ever to be applied in the world;
(*c*) to endow the family by children's allowances;

(d) to undertake both in the public and private sector a massive programme of investment, amounting to a general re-equipment of sections of British industry and absorbing over 20% of the national income;

(e) to build 200,000 houses a year, year after year;

(f) to raise the school leaving age:

(g) to raise the volume of British exports to over 170% of their pre-war volume; and

(h) finally to pile on top of all that a rearmament programme of some £1,500 million a year,

well, you *will* strain the resources of the economy to their very limits. You *will* find that you have to use all sorts of controls to prevent resources being used up on inessentials: it *will* be a constant struggle to divert sufficient resources to exports to pay for all the imports that you will need. And you *will* gratefully accept any help from external sources that may be offered to you, especially in the early post-war years.

Not that it has been wrong, in my view, thus to drive the economy to the very limit. It was only by doing so that the all-important increase of production has been secured. Moreover, the problems and difficulties—acute though they have been and are—which this hard driving has thrown up have been the problems and difficulties of *growth*, instead of the incomparably more morbid symptoms of stagnation and decay. In fact, the only really grave difficulty has been, and is, the balance of external payments.

Even here, however, it is the consequences of world rearmament—rather than our own programme in itself—which are causing the difficulty of the balance of overseas payments to reappear just when it appeared to have been mastered. I do not want to minimise our balance of payment troubles in any way. Nevertheless, we must reject the view that this is some fatal Nemesis which now hangs over the British economy, and which must sooner or later bring us to ruin. What, after all, is the basic task which we have to perform in order to balance our overseas payments? We must set aside exports—both visible and invisible —to a sufficient value to pay for those imports, visible and invisible, which we decide to buy. We must give the provision of these indispensable exports priority over every other call on our productive resources, over-consumption, over-investment, and for that matter over-rearmament—for a nation must eat before it can fight. Who can possibly say that there is anything inherently impossible about doing that?

Of course, the actual problem in any given year is immensely more complex than this suggests. There are really two balance of payments questions to consider. First, the United Kingdom's balance with the rest of the world, and second, the sterling area's balance with the dollar world. Then again, it is not indispensable, or for that matter possible, to balance our payments exactly in each year. Fluctuations in the world situation are much too wide for that. After all, as recently as 1950 we not only balanced our payments, but added 1,612 million dollars to the gold reserves of the sterling area. In fact the question of the size of our reserves is extremely important. For with adequate reserves we can ride out bad years without having to make disturbing readjustments.

Nevertheless, and at bottom, it *is* a question of providing an adequate value of exports of all kinds to meet our imports bill. We did this amply in 1950. We were not doing it in the four immediately post-war years, and it would then have been very difficult for us to have done it. We did not do it again, owing largely I think, to world rearmament, in 1951. Unquestionably we *must* do it, taking one year with another, in the future.

How large the bill will be and what volume of exports we must set aside to meet it will depend, of course, on those increasingly famous, or notorious, things, 'the terms of trade,' i.e. on the prices we have to pay for our imports and the prices we can get for our exports. Undoubtedly, if the terms of trade turned sufficiently against us, the burden of providing the necessary exports would become heavy indeed, and this would be a grave factor preventing our standard of life from rising as fast as it otherwise would. Some economists paint a gloomy prospect for us in this respect. They believe that the terms of trade are going to be permanently very adverse to us. If they mean that the terms of trade are not for a long while going to be so extremely favourable to us as they were in the nineteen-thirties, then I agree. But this is no disaster. After all, they never were anything like as favourable as that before the nineteen-thirties, and we managed all right. And I doubt not only whether they will ever be so favourable again, but even whether they ever ought to be—for in the 'thirties the terms of trade represented a real and in the end mutually disastrous exploitation of the primary producers. But if the economists mean that the terms of trade are going to go on getting worse and worse, then I do not believe that there is any real reason why they should. No doubt they may do so if the industrial nations do not make a sustained effort to help the primary producers of the under-developed world—and I should take it kindly if the word 'groundnuts' came into the reader's head at this point. But so long as we face up to that necessity of the world-wide development of primary production, I cannot see that there is any need to panic about the terms of trade. This necessity for the development of the undeveloped world is one aspect of the theme of the second part of this essay.

In any case, I believe that the worst that can happen to us in this respect is that relatively adverse terms of trade may prove a very serious drag on the rate at which we can raise our standard of life.

At what pace, then, *can* we expect to raise our standard of life if we can continue to keep our economic system running at full blast? It all depends, of course, on the rate at which our total production is rising and will rise. And that is a highly controversial question. The Government's *Digest of Statistics* informs us that physical production—the material products of industry and agriculture—have been increasing by more than 5% a year cumulative. (In itself, remember, that gives an increase of 100% in 14 years.) Moreover, the largest increase took place in 1950 over 1949, well after the productive system had been fully redeployed and there was no more labour to re-absorb from war industries and the forces. Therefore, one might suppose that there had been an increase not only of production, but also of *productivity* of this order of magnitude. But such a conclusion is hotly disputed. Many economists and statisticians declare that on the contrary productivity is only rising slowly. Apparently they consider that the 'invisible' output of those of us who are not engaged in material production has fallen so much that it is nearly offsetting the rise in the output of the 'material' industries. I find it hard to believe that all professional people have suddenly become much less efficient: that administrators are administrating, journalists writing, clerks clerking, writers writing and Members of Parliament talking far slower than ever before. As, however, no one has yet found a satisfactory method of measuring such non-material output, the discussion is likely to be a barren one. Nevertheless, it is true that one cannot assume that if physical output is going up at the rate of 5% a year, we shall all get 5% a year richer. Even apart from the tangled statistical issue about productivity, it depends on many factors—on the population trend, on whether we continue to put aside the same amount for capital development, on whether we distribute the national income in the same way, and on the question of whether a further turn for the worse in the terms of trade might make us have to set aside more for export.

No doubt any of these factors *might* have an adverse effect. What is there to set against these uncertainties and anxieties? We can set up against them the major factor of the present pace of technical progress. And my own belief is that the pace of technical progress is now so hot, that in spite of everything a remarkable increase in the standard of life is possible for us over say, two decades of peace—if, *but only if*, we keep our economy going at full blast.

No doubt many socialists—and not only socialists—have in the past exaggerated the growth in our powers of production. 'The problem of production has been solved' proved to be a very premature slogan. As soon as a reasonable degree of the redistribution of income had broken the artificial barriers restricting demand, millions of consumers turned out to have a more or less unlimited 'propensity to consume'—to use the Keynesian phrase. We now know that people will *consume* all right as soon as they are given half a chance to do so. But have we not now gone to the other extreme? Modern methods of production really are pretty remarkable. I cannot doubt that productivity will in fact rise fast and far, if only we continue to give the economy its head. After all, we have no experience of what it would mean to keep modern methods of production going at full blast over, say, a decade and a half of peace. Latter-day capitalism only worked by fits and starts, and never at anything like full power. No, when all the ifs and buts have been taken into account, I believe that there is a prospect of economic progress before us, such as we have never known; always provided that we continue boldly to correct the fatal tendency of our economy to so marked an internal unbalance that the wheels of production can hardly move.

But—it will be asked—has not the loss of Labour's hold upon the executive condemned us to a return to precisely the old situation of extreme social unbalance, with its fatal economic consequences of glut, stagnation and mass unemployment at home, together with attempts at renewed imperialist domination abroad? Has the prospect of steady and cumulative progress become illusionary with the return of the Conservatives to office?

I have no doubt that the instinctive *intentions* of the controlling forces of the Conservative Party are to reproduce as exactly as possible the social and economic pattern of the inter-war period. The only thing they really believe in is a good old-fashioned dose of deflation—as a means to the restoration of the former order of things.

Unquestionably that is what they would like to do: that is what all their guides, philosophers and friends, from Mr. Geoffrey Crowther to the simplest-minded broker, used to insist that they must do: that is the thing they believe in.

But will they really dare to deflate? When one envisages the probable industrial, social and political consequences of an attempt to meet our present problems by the deflationary method, one can hardly see a Conservative Government with a small majority embarking upon it. What, then, will they do? If they dare not apply the solutions on which they rely, what *will* they attempt? That is a question for them to answer. For our part, we may legitimately conclude that it is much too soon to suppose that the essentials of what has been accomplished in these six years of Labour rule are about to be destroyed. The power of the Labour Movement both within and without the House of Commons will be very great indeed. Wisely used, it can preserve the essence of the Labour achievement intact.

Moreover, if the Conservative Government is stopped, not only by our opposition, but by the whole social and economic climate of the period, from doing what it really believes in, it is unlikely that it will find any but the most temporary expedients with which to meet our national problems. In such a situation the prognosis for the Conservative administration can hardly be favourable.

This is not the place to consider the answers to our national problems which the next Labour administration will have to provide. Suffice it to say that the next Labour Government will have to combine great boldness with great firmness. For it is now evident from experience that, as had always been predicted would be the case, inflation is the besetting difficulty of the new, full-employment economy, just as deflation was the curse of our previous arrangements. Indeed, critics—both of the right and of the left—of our new arrangements often predict their collapse from an inability to prevent a continuous and accelerating rise in the price level, with all the disastrous consequences which such a process must ultimately have.

I do not myself believe for a moment that the unmistakable fact that a full employment economy generates powerful inflationary forces is a fatal defect: it is a *bias* in the new system which must be identified and vigorously counteracted. But granted that this is done, there is nothing fatal about it. But it does mean that every Chancellor, of every political hue, in a full employment economy will be confronted with a tendency for the total of money incomes to exceed the value of the goods and services available for consumption. And unless this tendency is firmly and adequately counteracted, there will appear balance of payment deficits, weakness of the pound, continual demands for revision of the social services as the cost of living rises, industrial disputes, and all the other discomforts, and ultimately disasters, of inflation.

The habitual posture of the Chancellor of the Exchequer in a full employment economy will be that of a man pulling and hauling with might and main at the brake levers of the economy. It will not be a very popular or comfortable posture. But what of that? It is his job! And granted that he does it, I see no reason why a community so mature and knowledgeable as our own should allow a full employment economy to wreck itself upon the rock of uncontrolled inflation.

The first task of the next Labour administration must, therefore, be to keep the tightest of tight hands upon all the levers of control, both physical and fiscal, which can be used to prevent total demand markedly exceeding output. For this is a condition of the satisfactory solution of all our economic problems—and of the problem of the maintenance of the necessary level of exports above all. But this, of course, is only the negative, protective side of the task of the next Labour administration. This it must do to prevent the new economy created between 1945 and 1951 from wrecking itself: and it remains to be seen how far down the inflationary path we may have slipped before Labour has an opportunity to apply again its characteristic anti-inflationary measures. For I fear that a Conservative administration will, in spite of its protestations, provide but weak barriers in this respect. In any case, it is the imperishable service of Sir Stafford Cripps that he faced with superb political courage the inherent necessity for a Labour Chancellor to combat inflation, whenever the tendencies of the new system threatened to get out of hand.

But all this fiscal firmness must be matched by an equal boldness. Our present social and economic arrangements are essentially transitional. We must push on to socialism or, inevitably, in the end we shall be pushed back to unreformed, pre-war, capitalism. What then will prove to be the best, most practicable and most direct road forward? I have recently suggested in a pamphlet called *The Just Society* that the movement should carefully examine the new ideas being put forward in many quarters for the transformation of our basic existing productive units, the joint stock companies. It may be that the swiftest progress towards socialism can be made, not by fusing these existing productive teams into great centralised public corporations, but by drastically altering their very nature. After all, what is the matter with the joint stock company is the irresponsible dictatorship exercised over it, nominally by its shareholders, actually in many cases by one or two self-appointing and self-perpetuating directors. Make public companies directly responsible both to the community and to the whole body of those engaged in their activities, and they would become institutions of a very different kind. This is the issue discussed by Mr. Austen Albu, who has given it careful attention in another essay in this volume.

I am far from suggesting that such a line of advance should supersede our familiar measures of public ownership—whether national, municipal or co-operative. But it does seem that there is here something worthy of close attention. Indeed, there is a remarkable convergence of opinions towards this concept, both within and without the Labour Movement. The danger is that unless socialists apply themselves closely to working out something really effective and drastic in this field, the whole idea will peter out in futile, and indeed often definitely bogus, schemes of co-partnership, with which we have long been familiar. But, in socialist hands, I believe that there is something really big to be done in this field.

Be all that as it may, the essential thing is that the Labour Movement should lead the country boldly forward towards socialism. If it did not, all that has been won in the last six years would in the end be lost again.

Indeed, some of our critics—particularly on the left—are inclined to suggest that in any case our new arrangements are inherently precarious in the extreme. They suggest that even if the next Labour administration were to combine firmness with boldness in the most felicitous manner, yet the maintenance and development of our new arrangements would be beset with international and internal hazards so grim as to make its survival unlikely.

No doubt it may be so. Optimism or pessimism about the future is so much a matter of temperament, and of what particular prognosis will suit one's own personal desires—whether conscious or unconscious—that the survival value of particular social arrangements over the longer term is apt to prove a barren subject of discussion. But this much, surely, it is possible to say. Our only chance as a community is to go forward along this road. Our new economy may be very precarious: but it is also very precious. I cannot really imagine the Britain of to-day being governed successfully under any other arrangements. In other words, disaster for Britain must result from attempts either to go back to unreformed capitalism or to plunge into full socialism by Leninist methods.

It is not, perhaps, unfair to remind those of our critics, who express the most emphatic doubts about our new economy, of all this when they tend to denigrate the achievement—modest enough though it may be—of 1945–51. For they inevitably tend to divert us from the one road forward for Britain which is not manifestly impassable.

And so much is at stake! Far more is at stake than whether our national standard of life should steadily rise over the next two decades. For if we do *not* continue the social and economic policies which will alone enable it so to rise, not only will the old symptoms of glut, mass unemployment and stagnation at home reappear, but also, and far worse, the old need to monopolise this or that part of the world as *our* market or *our* field of investment will be with us again. In that event the nation will be only too likely to attempt to retread that imperialist road which the Labour Government left decisively when it recognised the independence of India, Pakistan, Ceylon and Burma. And the imperialist road leads only to world war.

Part II

This last consideration brings me to the second part of this essay. It brings me to the problem of the *external* unbalance between different nations and parts of the world; and from that to a consideration of contemporary imperialism.

The first part of the essay has been devoted to showing that what was basically wrong *within* each national capitalism was an unbalance between the social groups and interests; it was the resultant maldistribution of income which produced the morbid symptoms of mass unemployment, under-investment and general stagnation. In Britain this *internal* unbalance has been largely corrected, and the morbid symptoms have duly disappeared. But capitalism as a whole—capitalism considered not within each nation but throughout its part of the world— exhibits another and perhaps even more dangerous lack of balance. This second unbalance is the extreme discrepancy between the rates of development of the different nations. This *external* unbalance has now become extreme. For the United States alone has not been injured in either world war. In size and strength the economy of the United States now towers above any other national capitalist system. I have already given figures showing the rate at which United States production has increased. The result is that the United States to-day consumes, for example, 50% of the world's output of copper, lead, zinc and tin; 60% of the world's aluminium and 75% of the world's wood pulp.[1] Moreover it is now proposed to increase the gross national product of the United States from the rate of $300 billion at the end of 1950, by a further 15% or $45 billions in the next three years—quite a reasonable rate of increase. And as a matter of fact, figures for March, 1951, showed deliveries to the home market at a rate 15% above March, 1950—though *that* rate of increase must only be a temporary one.

Now—and this is the essence of the matter—left to itself,

[1] I am indebted to Harold Wilson's address to the Fabian Conference on June 23rd, 1951, for these figures.

such a discrepancy in sheer size as now exists between the economy of the United States and all other economies would be bound to grow continually more extreme. Far from catching up, the rest of the capitalist world would continue to develop much more slowly than America: the gap would continually widen. Capitalism left to itself necessarily tends to work on the principle of 'to him that hath shall be given.'

True, the system has always had a method of attempting to overcome these discrepancies between the economies of different nations. It has had the method of the export of capital; the method of foreign investment on private account and for profit. As masses of capital accumulated in the one or two most advanced nations, it was lent to or directly invested in the less developed or undeveloped parts of the world.

Socialists have always considered this process to be the economic root of imperialism. For the great organisations of foreign investment, themselves increasingly monopolistic at home, and acting through their respective governments, sought to monopolise the remaining fields of profitable investment abroad. This form of overseas expansion led, much more than did the mere export of commodities, to the extension of the actual sovereignty of what we may call the capital exporting or 'metropolitan' nations over the areas into which their investors sank their capital. The whole world became increasingly 'colonialised', for only so could the investors be assured of the safety of their capital. It is above all this method which has led to the partitioning and then the re-partitioning of the globe, and so to those frightful collisions between the major industrial metropolises which we know as the first and second world wars.

No socialist—no sane citizen—can wish to see this method of the redistribution of capital through the world re-established. Yet let us face this fact: this has been, hitherto, the *only* known method by means of which the ever accumulating capital of the industrial metropolises could be spread through the world. Again, this method of moving accumulated capital across national frontiers by means of the pull of a higher rate of profit could not, I think, be restored even if we wished it to be. The world to-day is too inhospitable a place for the old-fashioned type of foreign investor: the whole mental climate of our times is inimical to this type of enterprise.

Nevertheless—and this is the essential point—let us not overlook the fact that if the thing cannot be done in the old way, some new way of doing it simply must be found.

Nothing is more certain than that breakdown must await all efforts to build a workable economy for the Western world, unless *some* way can be found of transferring the large masses of capital which rapidly accumulate in the one or two highly developed metropolises across national frontiers. Some way simply must be found by which this accumulated capital can be used to develop—not without reasonable return—the undeveloped or lagging parts of the world. For unless a way of doing this can be found, unless, in a word, we can find a substitute for imperialism, the already enormous discrepancies and disproportions—the huge *external* unbalance between different parts of the world—will get entirely out of hand. A small fraction of the human race would in that event begin to suffer again from the old morbid symptoms of a plethora of capital, while at the same time by far the larger part of the human race would remain sunk in destitution, condemned to primitive and capital-starved methods of production.

This crucial problem of the transfer of capital across national frontiers has arisen during these six post-war years in two distinct, though related, parts. There has been first of all a problem of the revival of the now secondary, yet still very important, industrial metropolises, Britain, France, Germany, the rest of Western Europe and Japan. All of them were in varying degrees shattered by the second world war. They would have had the greatest difficulty in reviving their economies without capital imports from the great industrial metropolis of metropolises, the United States, which alone has been actually increasing its accumulation throughout the whole period.

In the past this problem would have been met by raising

loans from private investors in the United States. This is how it *was* met after the first world war: the revival of the German economy, for instance, in the nineteen-twenties was almost entirely based upon the raising of ordinary commercial loans in the United States. This time nobody even supposed that that was a possible method. In the event, as we all know, the problem was met by the Marshall Plan. Substantial amounts of American capital resources were transferred to the other industrial metropolises of the non-Soviet world. (The original offer included Russia and her dependants, and it was Russia who opted out of the Plan, let it be remembered.) This was done either under the Marshall Plan itself or under similar arrangements. Some of the capital was exported as a free gift, some of it carries a moderate fixed rate of interest. The capital was not raised voluntarily from individual American investors, but was provided by the American Government out of taxation, i.e. it was compulsorily levied on the American taxpayers. And we ought not to forget this remarkable fact, for whatever was the mixture of motives in the doing of it, no other country has ever done anything of the kind before. By the end of 1950 this remarkable salvage operation had largely succeeded. The secondary industrial metropolises were going concerns again.

It is in this wider context that we must see our acceptance of Marshall Aid. And it is equally in this context that we must put our own rendering of a nearly equal quantity of aid to countries far worse hit than ourselves immediately after the war. In those years there was nothing in the least wrong or 'weak' in the acceptance of such aid. It was a generous and imaginative act on the part of the United States to proffer it, and it was necessary for the secondary industrial centres to accept it, if the truly frightful unbalance between them and the United States which the second world war had caused was to be even mitigated. But by 1950 *this* particular external unbalance—the unbalance *between* the different industrial countries—had been largely brought under control. True, it is breaking out again today—as a result of world-wide rearmament. But in general the period of the need to transfer help from the main industrial centre

—the United States—to the secondary countries is over. In particular we in Britain must in future stand on our own feet as a going concern. This period is being succeeded by another period in which the problem of the transfer of capital across frontiers will arise in a different way, *and on a far greater scale*. For the problem will be that of the transfer of capital *from* the industrial countries taken together to the vast undeveloped areas of the world: to Asia, Africa and South America. But before going on to that major question we ought to make up our minds as socialists what we really think about and feel about what we may call the Marshall Aid period.

It may not be without interest to consider the views of the Yugoslav statesman, M. Djilas, in this connection. In a recent article in *Borba* (a Yugoslav newspaper) for November 26th, 1950, Djilas sets out the problem. He writes that the second world war, 'ruined the productive forces of Europe to a tremendous extent. But the very same war pushed productive forces in the United States to unprecedented heights. The result was a profound economic gulf between the U.S.A. and the remainder of the world.' 'Leading American circles', he considers, saw that this extreme unbalance must produce 'serious economic upheavals and an economic crisis' in the United States itself; that this would be 'catastrophic for the world,' and that there was no hope of meeting the situation by the old methods of the export of capital on private account and for profit. In Djilas's words, 'so long as the world remained as they found it, with the exportation of capital as the basic form of economic and other expansion', the difficulty was insoluble. So the American leaders had to do something about it, he considers; and what they did was to think up and put into operation 'unpaid-for aid'. 'This aid first began to appear', he writes, 'more or less extensively during, and at the close of, the second world war (Lend-Lease, UNRRA) while since the war it has been further continued in various forms (the Marshall Plan).'

The American leaders preferred to do this giving away, Djilas continues. 'For what profit would it be to the capitalists to have a superfluity of goods (or of capital) without any purchasers? What profit to be able to make machinery but not to sell it? It was at least better to give away products than to burn them or throw them into the sea; if only with an eye to the future their commodity nature could be retained.'

No doubt there is some force in this attribution of fear of an internal glut and slump as the motive of successive American foreign aid programmes. But taken by itself it strikes me as one-sided. After all, through the 'thirties America *did* prefer, precisely, to burn or 'plough under' her unsaleable surplus products rather than to give them away. It marks a real revolution in American opinion that they are now giving them away. No doubt one of the main reasons for that mental revolution, as well as the fear of glut, is fear of Russia. The truth is that the existence of an alternative social system has made the whole of the Western world feel that it simply cannot and must not let there be another major slump of the 1929–31 order ever again. But when all that is allowed for it is surely wrong to overlook the reality of the idealistic and humanitarian impulses which moved the American people, and which alone enabled their Government to act in the enlightened way it did.

In any case, Djilas comes to the conclusion that the Lend-Lease, UNRRA, Marshall Aid, and now, he might have added, the Foreign Aid and Point Four, forms of the transfer of capital *from* the industrial metropolises where it accumulates, across frontiers, *to* the places where it is desperately needed, is for the present at least, the main form which this indispensable economic operation takes.

Djilas asks the question: Is this 'Marshall Aid' type of the transfer, or export, of capital a form of imperialism? His answer appears to be that, yes, it is: but that it is a new, mild and etiolated form of imperialism. It carries with it some elements of subjection and exploitation to the receiving country, he considers, but far less than any other previous form of imperialism. In fact, it tends to break up the old colonial systems, which were much more exploitative. Finally he favourably contrasts this type of contemporary American economic expansion with the

Russian post-war expansion, and with the Russian treatment of the Eastern European countries which have been brought into the Russian orbit.

He has some extremely harsh things to say of Russian methods in this connection. For instance, he writes:

> But where in this respect does the new, 'soviet' imperialism stand? Are there new developments in this too, such as those characteristic of the old private capitalist monopolies? All that is new here is the fact that the state which all, or nearly all, believed to be socialist, has through its own internal state capitalist development, turned into an imperialist power of the first order. But as for the actual forms, through the relatively poor development of its forces of production, what characterises this new, state-capitalist, imperialism is precisely that it has the old, colonial-conquest imperialist forms accompanied, albeit, in 'socialist' uniforms, by the old political relations: the export of capital is accompanied by a semi-military occupation, by the rule of an official caste and the police, by the strangling of any democratic tendencies, by the establishment of obedient governments, by the most extensive corruption and by unscrupulous deception of the working people.

Before we reject this verdict on Russia's treatment of the countries for which she forms the capital exporting metropolis, we should recall that Djilas has actually experienced the thing, while we have not.

Djilas therefore concludes that the American type of post-war economic expansion is imperialistic, but that it is a much superior and less exploitative type of imperialism, as compared both to any previous imperialism and, notably, as compared to the contemporary Russian way of attempting to do the same thing. He concludes that in the successive external aid programmes America found a way of making those indispensable transfers of capital across frontiers without which the Western world would have come to grief.

For my part, it seems to be stretching language very far indeed to call a process by which capital is largely given away, even though the giver thereby inevitably acquires some measure of influence and control over the recipients, a form of imperialism. Is not the real question rather one of whether the American people can be expected to continue to tax themselves for this purpose?

We certainly cannot expect them—and do not even desire them—to go on taxing themselves in this way for *our* benefit. Except possibly for the special case of rapid rearmament—which after all America herself is urging on us—*we must not take any more American help*. We must, I repeat, set aside the volume of exports necessary to balance our external payments, taking one year with another, as an almost absolute priority, taking precedence over all other demands on our national product. Moreover, the other secondary industrial metropolises must, and surely can, also stand on their own feet in the fairly near future. The speed of their revival is now rapid.

No, it is not in order to provide further aid to ourselves that the American people may be asked to tax themselves in future. It is rather to join with us, as the senior partner, in a joint endeavour of unprecedented magnitude to develop the under-developed continents. And, with respect for Comrade Djilas, it would be a great pity to call them 'imperialists'—of however enlightened a kind—if they do so.

For the revival of the secondary industrial centres is only the first and smaller of the two things which have got to be done if the Western world is to go forward, reasonably in balance and as a whole. As soon as the other industrial metropolises have been got going, it is indispensable that they and the United States together should turn to the far vaster business of pouring capital into the relatively undeveloped parts of the world—into, essentially, Asia, Africa and South America. That is the real and gigantic job that has got to be done if we are to make our world work. It has got to be done not only, and even in a sense not principally, because of strictly economic considerations. Not only will the economic unbalance of the world get out of hand, but intolerable political consequences will certainly ensue unless we can find ways of steadily developing the vast pre-capitalist areas of the world. From China to Peru the great majority of the human race is still but slightly touched by the Industrial Revolution. But, psychologically, politically, they are waking up: and unless acceptable ways and means of enabling them to develop their countries can be found they will certainly be lost to the Western world. They will pass into the Russian orbit—into the orbit, that is to say, of a far less highly developed industrial metropolis which can do far less for them economically.

The American Government, just before Korea, was turning its attention to this—the basic world problem. By annunciating Point Four of the Truman Programme, it sought to prepare the American people for an unprecedented feat of political imagination and overseas economic enterprise, without hope of high material reward in the short run. Since then the Korean war has touched off the rearmament programme of the Western world. To some extent this must postpone the implementation of a Point Four type of programme for the publicly controlled and directed export of capital to the under-developed world. But it need not—in fact, it *must* not— postpone it for more than a year or so. For such a programme is a necessity—both an economic and a political necessity—if our part of the world is to be made to work.

Meanwhile, the rearmament programme, burdensome as it is for us, is, curiously enough, by no means all loss to the under-developed continents. For these are the areas of the production of the main raw materials and primary products. And as we know to our cost, world-wide rearmament has sent the prices of these raw materials and primary products sky-high. The turn of the terms of trade *against* the industrial metropolises and in favour of the primary producers, which is for us the most costly feature of rearmament, is pouring money into the hands of the primary producers. It is true that they may find difficulty in spending that money on the capital resources which they need, since the industries of Britain and America in particular are so heavily committed. But this will be a passing phase, and, moreover, the revival of several other industrial centres, notably Germany and Japan, which are not engaged on rearmament, means that the under-developed areas may even now find it possible to spend their big takings effectively on industrial imports. (Germany's exports actually doubled last year, I understand.)

However, this is merely an often overlooked by-product of rearmament. In the long run nothing will do but the conscious direction by the governments of all the industrial metropolises of the export of substantial masses of capital to the undeveloped areas of the world. If we can do this the Western world will work; if not, not.[1]

To sum up the argument of both parts of the essay. A shift of power away from a narrow and monopolistic group towards the people has occurred to a lesser or greater extent in the main Western industrial metropolises—most perhaps in Britain; least in, say, Italy. This has been enough to force capitalism to devote itself to a significant degree to using its resources to raising the general standard of life. There has been a redistribution of the national income and a development of agriculture. This has largely removed the old morbid symptoms of glut and stagnation. For these were symptoms of the internal unbalance of the social classes within each national capitalism. A reanimation of these economies has resulted. A remarkable prospect of economic progress, with a general and steady raising of the standard of life, appears to be opening up before us in Britain—if, but only if, our economy is not allowed to slip back into its old unbalance.

But this was only one of the essential unbalances of capitalism. The other was, and is, the ever-growing disproportion between the development of the different industrial metropolises, and still more between these industrial metropolises taken together and the undeveloped parts of the world. These disproportions, which in the case of the United States have now reached an

[1] Mr. Colin Clark told me, in conversation, just before the Korean War that he and his fellow statistical economists calculated that it would be from about 1955 onwards that the necessity to move really large masses of capital from the industrial metropolises to the undeveloped areas would arise.

extreme degree, can only be dealt with by the transfer to the undeveloped world of large quantities of capital by, primarily, the United States, but also by the other industrial centres, as they revive. The old method of exporting capital on private account, with all its fatal imperialist consequences, neither should, nor for that matter can, be revived.

What then can be put in its place? *Only a publicly controlled and directed export of capital.* Examples of this are afforded by the American foreign aid programme. These programmes have achieved a remarkable degree of success in reviving the secondary industrial metropolises. But this phase is nearly over. For the future, if we are to make a success of the Western world, the United States will have to join with us in a sustained effort to develop the undeveloped continents. If, but only if, this can be done there is no reason why a period of great and stable progress should not lie ahead of the Western world.

What political conclusions are suggested by this analysis? The question of the hour is whether the key countries of the world will recognise that a possibility of unprecedented economic progress now exists, and will be willing to work for it —or at least, not to work against it. If Britain and America will seize this chance, and if Russia will at least recognise its existence, it will not fail. In that event we shall avoid world war, in the only way that it can be avoided in the long run—namely, by maintaining a peace that is genuinely tolerable and possible for the peoples of the world.

Let us look at the thing from the point of view of Russia, America and Britain in turn. Take the Russian angle first.

There is now little possibility that Russia will ever *take part* with us in any great programme of world development of this kind—as for a moment she seemed willing to do when she came to Paris at the initiation of the Marshall Plan.

I have always thought that that Russian walk-out—however inevitable it now seems to us to have been—marked the decisive turn towards the Cold War. As it happens, I was seeing Ernest Bevin in his room at the Foreign Office on the morning that the first news that the Russians would come to the Conference was received. Bevin was deeply stirred by it. I had come to discuss some Food Ministry problem with him. But he kept saying, 'Perhaps they *will* play after all.' A few days later the Russians went home and pulled the wretched Czechs after them. But that is now all water under the bridge. The most that is now possible—and this is all that is necessary—is that the Russian Government will recognise the possibility, and the actual beginning, of progressive development in the Western world.

Curiously enough, the leading Russian economist, Professor Varga, at the very outset of the post-war period, *did* recognise all this. Varga saw and wrote that in the West the power of that tiny section of monopolists whose interests had conflicted with *all* expansion between the wars had been shaken: that democratic pressure in the West bid fair to push capitalism, however unwillingly, along the road of raising the general standard of life and developing agriculture. (I am not aware whether he dealt with the next problem of finding new, non-imperialist forms for the transfer of capital across frontiers to the under-developed continents.) He held that it would be rash for the Russian Government to assume any early Western collapse or slump of the pre-war kind: he concluded that democratic pressure was making of Western capitalism a going concern, at least for the present period. And his implication was obviously that Russia must be prepared to 'co-exist' with this going concern for the time being: that it would be rash indeed to try to 'break' such a system by head-on opposition.

I have no doubt that had the Politburo accepted Varga's thesis they would have been, if not co-operative, at least moderate and reserved in their opposition to the West in the past six years. For Stalin and his colleagues have always shown themselves willing to face facts, if only they can be convinced of the existence of the facts. But the Politburo did not accept Varga's thesis. On the contrary, he lost his job—though not his head—and had to recant utterly. That meant that the Politburo had taken its stand on the view that nothing had really changed in Western capitalism: that the New Deals and

Fair Deals in America, the central planning, nationalisations, redistribution of the national income, social services—the Welfare State—in Britain, and the less marked, but perceptible, corresponding measures in Western Europe, were all quite negligible: that just the same forces as before were at work: that capital would accumulate in great unmanageable piles at the centre: that the standard of life, and so power to consume, of the population would be held down: that slump and crisis at the centre and a feverish drive to imperialist expansion at the peripheries would quickly reappear.

On such a view Russian policy since the war is thoroughly comprehensible. 'How *can* we "co-exist" with such a system?' the Politburo no doubt concluded. 'It is inherently incapable of co-existing peacefully with anyone. We must utilise every hour to strengthen our power for the coming clash of arms: at all costs we must fortify the Socialist bastion, Bolshevise our satellites, and weaken the imperialists from within. No matter what the sacrifices, no matter how aggressive we appear to the world, we must at all costs strengthen ourselves. For, as we alone can foresee, the inherent nature of their system will before long leave the imperialists no option but to attack us.'

We can but adjure the Politburo in the words of that great English revolutionary, Oliver Cromwell: 'I beseech you, in the bowels of Christ, think it possible you may be mistaken.' If only the members of the Politburo will cease to believe that they possess an exclusive and infallible revelation, which absolves them from looking at the facts of the world about them, they will see that things are not going according to their preconception. They will see that the democratic forces in the West have modified the traditional development of capitalism: that if Russia continues to act as if nothing in the West had changed, only a head-on collision can result. Of course we cannot prove that the democratic forces and parties in the West will succeed in making things go their way—any more than the Politburo can prove that they will succeed in their vast and still hazardous reconstruction of the basis of the Russian economy—though from what indications one can get, that development too is going ahead fairly effectively. We need not despair, however, that in the end the Politburo will take account of the real facts; for they respect facts, just as they respect resistance—and they are encountering resistance. We can only hope that certain recent indications mean that they are at least beginning to review their disastrously schematic, and therefore basically mistaken, appreciation of Western development.

Now let us look at the contemporary scene from the American angle. Whether or not we avoid the third world war will be partly determined by the degree to which America is able to do two very difficult things—the one in the short run, the other in the long. In the short run she will need to show extraordinary patience combined with firmness. If peace is to be saved, America must show herself capable of neither yielding nor attacking. And that will not come easily to the American temperament. For a number of years the West must simply 'man the walls'. Peace can be preserved, but only if the Russian leaders find, as a fact of experience, that the West is both completely firm and completely unaggressive.

But this is only the first and easier part of the job. We must be strong not only in the military sphere—though that is indispensable in the short run. In the long run, it is not merely, or even mainly, the outer military crust of the West which we must prove to be firm and solid. It is above all the inner economic, social and political heart of the West which we must prove to be sound and viable.

And this is the second difficult enterprise in which America must play a part commensurate to her position in the world. In the long run no amount of American or anyone else's rearmament, no thousands of atom bombs, no hundreds of divisions, no production of tanks or aircraft by the hundreds of thousands, will save the West, unless it continues to find a way of making its economic system work. That, I repeat again, means turning our marvellous productive resources on to the task of steadily, and to an indefinite extent, raising the standard of life of the whole population of our world. And that in turn, and above all in the case of America, but also for ourselves, means finding a way of regularly transferring great amounts of capital, as they accumulate, across national frontiers, from the industrial centres to the undeveloped parts of the world. It can be done—but it is no small task. It will not do itself; the old method of profit-seeking overseas investment on private account can never again fill the bill. Great and continuing programmes on Point Four lines, directed to Asia, Africa and South America, are indispensable to the salvation of our world. Britain must play her full part in them—but the greater part of the capital can come only from the United States. It is a vast, difficult but surely inspiring, mission which faces the American people.

Finally, let us look at the world scene from our own British angle. I cannot doubt what is the British task and mission. It is in Britain that the democratic forces have really got a grip on the economy and begun to transform its nature. It is here that the democratic forces have been solidly united in one political party which has had the executive in its control for six consecutive years. It is here that the technique of contemporary central planning, either by means of physical controls or Keynesian fiscal means, is best understood. It is here that the redistribution of the national income, and the turning of the economy to its true task of steadily raising the general standard of life, has been carried farthest.

And everything, I repeat once again, turns on this. Unless this is done—and preserved—the Politburo has *not* miscalculated. It is only to the extent that this is accomplished that the Western world can become progressive or even viable. To the extent that this is *not* done all the old, morbid, fatal tendencies to glut, slump and crisis at home, and to aggressive imperialism abroad, will reappear. And to-day such imperialist tendencies could not fail to produce the third world war.

Our task is, then, to preserve, to perfect, to extend our newly developing social and economic system. Our national mission is to carry through the peaceful social revolution which we have begun. *Unless* we can do these things we have nothing very special to say to the world in this second half of the twentieth century. *If* we can do them we can lead the world by our example. Pericles said that Athens must make herself 'the education of Hellas'. It is surely not wrong for us to aspire, in all humility, to play some such role in the West to-day. We shall not do it, of course, by preaching at other peoples; probably the less we say about what we are doing the better in the long run. Sooner or later what is being accomplished here will be apparent to the world and we shall not lack imitators.

Therefore our supreme role is to stick to it. We have made no more than a beginning: but it is a good beginning and it can be indefinitely extended. True, our political opponents will always seek to undo some at least of what we have done. That is natural enough and we can meet them in fair political fight.

Nor should we do anything but welcome those critics in our own ranks who urge us to go faster and farther. There is a constant danger of stagnation and complacency in any huge and powerful movement such as ours. But when we remember what is at stake, how can we avoid impatience with that small section of opinion which tells us that everything that British Labour has so far accomplished is 'really' no good; that nothing has 'really' been changed: that, anyhow, we are all inevitably drifting to world disaster: that *we* are helpless, and that *everything* is hopeless? These defeatists are, whether they know it or not, at one with the Politburo in declaring that nothing can be altered save by world catastrophe. It is not true. In six years the shape and direction of the British economy *has* been altered. In the Labour Movement the British people have forged an unmatched instrument of continuing social change. It is our national task—our mission to the world—to develop, to sharpen and to use that instrument.